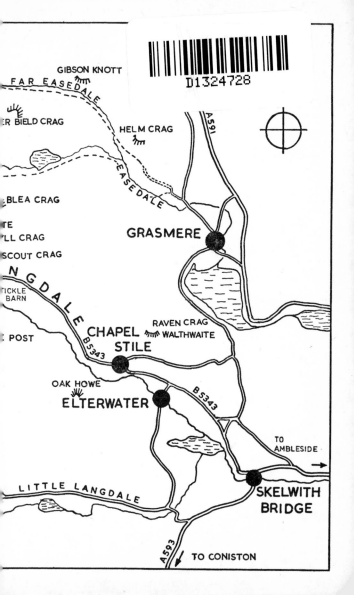

GIBSON KNOTT

FAR EASEDALE

ER BIELD CRAG

HELM CRAG

EASEDALE

BLEA CRAG

TE
LL CRAG

SCOUT CRAG

N GDALE

TICKLE
BARN

POST

GRASMERE

A591

RAVEN CRAG
WALTHWAITE

CHAPEL
STILE

B5343

OAK HOWE

ELTERWATER

B5343

LITTLE LANGDALE

TO
AMBLESIDE

SKELWITH
BRIDGE

A593

TO CONISTON

D1324728

Climbing Guides to the
English Lake District

Great
Langdale

by M. G. Mortimer

Edited by D. Miller

Published by the Fell and Rock Climbing Club
of the English Lake District

© ISBN 0 85028 0222

Previous Editions:

1926   George Basterfield
1938   William Clegg
1950   Arthur Dolphin and John Cook
1967   Allan Austin
1973   Allan Austin and Rod Valentine

Present edition: 1980

Printed by Joseph Ward & Co. (Printers) Ltd., Dewsbury,
West Yorkshire

CONTENTS

INTRODUCTION

This volume is the second of a new series of Rock Climbing Guides in process of publication by the Fell and Rock Climbing Club of the English Lake District.

Although it includes many additional new climbs, this guide is slimmer and more convenient than the previous edition, because of the economical style and layout adopted for the new series. This series will comprise five volumes, including the various areas as follows:

1. Buttermere, Newlands and Eastern Crags
2. Great Langdale
3. Scafell, Eskdale, Dunnerdale and Dow Crag
4. Pillar Rock and Great Gable
5. Borrowdale

Great Langdale is probably the most complete climbing area in the Lake District, with a choice of good routes of all standards, on crags varying from road-side to remote mountain locations. The valley continues to be popular and this is reflected by the considerable number of new climbs included in this guide, some of which are amongst the most difficult in the district.

I should like to thank Mike Mortimer, a prolific guidewriter, for the considerable time and effort needed to update and revise this volume. Heaton Cooper is again to be thanked for the use of his drawings and colour frontispiece, and Jill Aldersley for providing additional drawings.

D.E.M. 1980

General Note

The grading of the climbs in difficulty refers to ascents and to dry weather conditions, and is as follows:

Moderate	Severe
Difficult	Severe (hard)
Difficult (hard)	Very severe (mild)
Very difficult	Very severe
Very difficult (hard)	Very severe (hard)
Severe (mild)	Extremely severe (E1 to E5)

The Extremely severe grade is subdivided into five sections, from E1 for the easiest to E5 for the hardest extremes at the present time. In addition to the adjectival grade for overall grading, individual technical pitch grades have been included for climbs of Very severe (mild) grade and above. The technical pitch grades are an attempt at an objective assessment of the pure difficulty of the pitch. The technical pitch grades used are as follows:

4a, 4b, 4c; 5a, 5b, 5c; 6a, 6b.

A few routes still require a limited use of aid and this is indicated in the descriptions. Many aid reductions have been achieved in recent years and routes are described in the most free style in which they are known to have been climbed and they are graded accordingly.

A star system has been used to indicate routes of particular quality with three stars being reserved for excellent routes. The absence of stars does not mean that a climb is poor, unless it is described as such. Climbs which have not been repeated, or verified by the Guide writer are indicated by an obelisk (†) and their descriptions and gradings should be treated with caution.

The length given for each pitch indicates the length of climbing involved. The leader is advised not to stint himself of rope and should allow additional rope for belaying and waist lengths.

The angle of a glacis is such that it can be walked up; a slab is steeper, whilst a wall is nearly vertical and may overhang. The slopes are approximately below 30°, between 30° and 75°, above 75°. The location of a crag is indicated by its Ordnance Survey grid reference.

The terms 'true left' and 'true right' are used to describe the position of a crag in a valley or ghyll relative to the direction of flow of the stream.

The terms 'left' and 'right', unless otherwise stated, mean as the climber is facing his climb.

PREFATORY NOTE

This edition is a complete revision of the 1973 Langdale Guide by Allan Austin and Rodney Valentine, and many of the descriptions have been altered to take account of modern developments.

Nevertheless, I must acknowledge my debt to these and previous authors; my work is based on theirs. My thanks must also go to the authors of the recent FRCC publications of new climbs: Dave Armstrong, Pete Botterill, Pete Whillance, Ed Grindley and Martin Berzins; without their efforts the writing of this guide would have been a much more arduous task.

Grateful thanks are due to all those who have provided information and advice, solicited or otherwise. I would especially like to thank the following, who have helped me to check routes: Jane Moran, Steve Foster, Ken Wood, Jim Moran and Marjorie Allen. Finally, I would like to thank John Ridgeway for introducing me to Langdale climbing.

M.G.M. 1980

HISTORICAL

The history of any one climbing ground can never be regarded as a complete story in itself. Rather is it but one ingredient in the history of a whole district's climbing. Where, in the early days, a new climb, or even a new type of climb, was discovered on any one crag, that in itself showed the way to similar routes on other crags, or even to the exploitation of new crags where this newer type of climb was waiting to be led. And so the histories of all crags become but one all-embracing story. Nowhere has this been better demonstrated than in that excellent article by H. M. Kelly and J. H. Doughty in the *Fell and Rock Climbing Club Journal* of 1936. There it is shown how the original story of English rock-climbing is a story of summit seeking—of easy-way finding.

Langdale offered no such summits, no such easy ways. Langdale crags, Gimmer and Bowfell in particular, had their impressiveness —not one of broken, towering massiveness such as the Pillar and Scafell—but one of vast, airy smoothness, in no way inviting to the early pioneers. Little, too, was to be seen of the comfort of chimney and crack, beloved of the second group of our early climbers. But what little there was of this was duly noted by W. P. Haskett-Smith, most aptly named 'the prince of pioneers'. So in the 1880's he climbed the North-west Gully on Gimmer, the two Pavey Ark Gullies, and the North Gully of Bowfell Buttress. This was the real start of rock-climbing in Langdale, though Jack's Rake, probably known to shepherds from very early times, had been crossed within the previous decade by R. Pendlebury.

Perhaps, therefore, it would be unfair to say that Langdale lagged behind the other centres in its climbing history, although its first ascents came half-a-century later. More fairly one might say that Langdale took its true position in the story of English climbing, starting at the beginning of the 'Gully Epoch'. The remainder of the century completed this with the addition of the two Pavey Ark chimneys and a few outlying scrambles on Bowfell.

It was with the 'Slab and Wall' period that Langdale came into its own. The Langdale crags, Gimmer in particular, are perfect examples of this type. So, in the first decade of this century, the first climbs typical of Langdale began. H. B. Lyon and E. Rigby started the Gimmer alphabet. Bowfell Buttress climb and the Crescent on Pavey Ark opened up the two other main crags. From that time until the war, development in Langdale, though much of it was on outlying minor crags, went steadily ahead.
During the war activity ceased.

Then came the great boom period, and in addition to his exploits on other crags, G. S. Bower quickly added a round half-dozen routes in this area. His ascents of 'D' on Gimmer and Crescent Slabs on Pavey Ark advanced Langdale climbing by almost one full stage in severity. H. B. Lyon returned, seventeen years after his original ascents of 'B' and Lyon's Crawl, to add Bracket and Slab Climb, Chimney Buttress, and White Gill Chimney to the list.

In 1924 the first of the 'very severes' came from J. A. Wray with 'E' route, and M. de Selincourt, in addition to four new routes (climbed solo), added the second with his ascent of the Right-Hand Wall of Bowfell.

Two years later G. S. Bower again looked round the North-west Side of Gimmer, which he had opened out in 1920 with Ash-tree Slabs, and added Pallid Slabs and Hiatus. Then in their 'laudable attempt' to put G. Basterfield's newly published Langdale Guide quickly out of date, A. B. Reynolds, H. S. Gross, and G. G. Macphee added another three 'very severes' on this side. Reynolds' final ascent of the Crack was the culmination of a very determined siege of a most noteworthy route. So came into being what, for a short time, was known as the 'Gentlemen's Side' of Gimmer, in comparison with the easier and now much be-touristed routes on the other faces. But not for long did the North-west Face merit this title, for Miss N. Ridyard quickly had them all ticked off.

By now Gimmer had a veritable network of routes on all its faces—there seemed little room for more—though never let it be said that there *is* no room. However, subsequent exploration has been concerned mostly with other crags. In addition to routes on minor crags, four new routes have been added on the Bowfell crags, and two 'very severes', Deer Bield Crack in Far Easedale, and Stoats' Crack on Pavey Ark, have added greatly to the quality and prestige of Langdale climbing. The girdling of Gimmer has also been completed.

Today rock climbing enjoys more popularity than ever before. The number of its devotees has grown enormously in recent years, and Langdale—so easily accessible from the civilized part of the Lake District, therefore becomes perhaps *the* most popular playground for the sport. What new climbs will this great influx of climbers add to our sport—what new methods—what new developments? The next new guide to rock climbing in Langdale shall tell.

Wm. Clegg, 1938

1938-49

Langdale remains as popular a centre as ever, as witness the fact that the number of recorded climbs in the area has been more than doubled since the publication of the last Guide. Even during the war years activity was considerable, many finding the fells and crags ideally suited for precious leaves away from front-line England. Throughout this time the name of R. J. Birkett has figured prominently. His ascent of 'F' Route was probably the most notable achievement at a time when Gimmer still offered tantalising possibilities along natural weaknesses. Sydney Thompson and John Ashton, also contributed several fine routes here, but by the early 1940's interest almost inevitably began to be directed towards the further exploration of other crags. On Bowfell, the Buttress was 'girdled' but otherwise produced little of real merit.

Pavey Ark was rescued from its rather traditional status of a purely wet-weather cliff by the discovery of a number of good buttress climbs of all grades of difficulty, culminating in H. A. Carsten's magnificent Rake End Wall.

Despite this progress on the major crags, undoubtedly the most important feature of recent exploration in Langdale has been the development of White Ghyll and, to a lesser degree, of Raven Crag.

The former had already provided routes of quality in its classic Chimney and Slab climbs, but it was J. W. Haggas' epic ascent of the Gordian Knot which revealed the possibilities of the previously untouched, but extremely imposing, central mass. Five years elapsed before Birkett made the second ascent of this fine climb and then went on to pioneer a host of worthy routes along the entire range of the Crag, of which Haste Not and Perhaps Not rank among the best and hardest climbs in the district. The opening-out of Raven Crag was due in the main to the industry of A. Gregory, although Bilberry Buttress, perhaps the most attractive route here, was climbed quite early in the period by C. F. Rolland. The network of climbs now to be found on this crag is adequately justified by its extreme accessibility.

Among this spate of novelties the older routes have lost little of their warranted reputation. Established favourites, such as Gimmer Crack, may seem a trifle easier now that the trail is well blazoned; Right-Hand Wall has shed most of its legendary armour. The intrinsic difficulties of Deer Bield Crack, however, are as acute as ever, even if the most formidable problem in the district today is Kipling Groove.

In concluding his Historical note in 1938, Clegg pondered on the future of the sport in Great Langdale. Today the general standard of climbing is undoubtedly higher. New methods too (such as the carrying of pitons for use in emergency and a more scientific system of rope handling and belaying) have been introduced as safety measures, though they cannot be said directly to have influenced the recent exploration of the district. Future climbers will no doubt have their own story of further developments.

Arthur Dolphin and John Cook, 1950

1950-65

The most notable event of the post-war years was the first ascent of Kipling Groove. It was a remarkable lead for the time. Technically it was no harder than its contemporaries, but one faced the difficulties in a much more uncompromising position—and in those days there was no peg. At the time it seemed a fitting climax to a period of intense exploration.

Today we see it as the first of the big modern routes, a couple of years before its time perhaps, but setting a pattern for the future. It ushered in a new era and in the next few years was to be eclipsed by new developments in Langdale, and left far behind by the rapid rise in standards taking place outside the confines of the valley.

Nevertheless, measured by any yardstick, it was, and is, an outstanding climb, marking the emergence of Arthur Dolphin as possibly the finest leader of the period and opened the campaign that over the next few years was to make him a legend in his own lifetime.

This same period marked the retirement of another great climber. In White Ghyll, R. J. Birkett was closing down a fantastically prolific career, and for a brief period of two or three years the two men who had dominated the crags of the Lake District for so long raised the standard of Lakeland climbing to a level unequalled elsewhere in Britain.

The years following the appearance of the new guide were undoubtedly Dolphin's years. During this period extensive developments took place on most of the crags covered in this volume. The event of 1951 was the conquest—at last—of the famous central buttress on Deer Bield, thus solving one of the 'Last Great Problems' of the district, and at the same time producing a superb climb Later in the year a visit was paid to Bowfell and Rubicon Groove appeared—a bold initial lead. In 1952 in spite of activities in other districts, time was found for several first-rate routes, notable amongst which was Dunmail Cracks, in which the lead was shared with P. J. Greenwood. But best of all was a great route on Bowfell, the Sword of Damocles, comparable with Deer Bield Buttress. Again the honours were shared with Greenwood. The following year Arthur Dolphin, tragically, lost his life on the Géant thus bringing to an abrupt end one of the finest chapters in the history of Lakeland climbing.

The early fifties was also the time when East Raven enjoyed its burst of popularity. These little crags, stretching down from Raven Crag itself towards the New Dungeon Ghyll Hotel, had been by-passed by climbers of earlier generations. But now they became covered in a network of short routes reminiscent of gritstone climbs.

It is probably not true to say that the climbers concerned were alcoholics, but it is certain that the Old Hotel and its nearness to the crags was an important factor in explorations carried out at that time—and indeed, in climbing there today.

Climbing at the same time, but not directly concerned with the existing Langdale clientele was a new group of 'tigers' from Wales, the 'little men', the men of the Rock and Ice. In other districts these men proved to be the most formidable group of climbers ever to operate on British rock. In Langdale their offerings were less important than elsewhere—but notable for all that. Pendulum on Deer Bield was found, then Moseley returned with Whillans and the crag was girdled. Joe Brown led the unclimbed corner in White Ghyll and named it Laugh Not.

By far the most important event of the decade was the emergence of Pavey Ark as one of the most important climbing grounds of the Langdale area. This huge rambling mass of a crag, liberally endowed with heather and juniper, fostered an impression of decay. It was so different from the more obvious attractions of White Ghyll or Gimmer, but Pavey is big. It was easy to lose sight of a 200-foot buttress in this vast 800-foot crag. For many years both local and visiting tigers passed it by. It was left to the enthusiasts.

Arthur Dolphin was the first of the moderns to realise its possibilities. His activities elsewhere overshadow his Pavey contributions and one tends to forget that he made four routes here. These additions marked the opening of the Pavey renaissance.

The next generation appeared in the persons of Brian Evans and Allan Austin. Over the next few years new routes on the crag were exclusively the work of these two. About this time Joe Brown made one of his sporadic visits to the Lakes and produced Eliminot in White Ghyll. As a route it has few attractions, but it is an exceedingly fine piece of climbing. On Pavey Ark explorations pushed forward, helped for the next couple of years by a new name, Eric Metcalf.

Astra and Arcturus were superb discoveries in this period, but new routes were becoming difficult to find. Gradually they became less frequent. Existing classics were no less popular, and well-blazoned trails no less attractive, yet the load began to spread a little. It was time to take stock!

During work for the guidebook several odds and ends were discovered, Poacher and Gandalf's Groove seemed worthwhile. Gimmer String was cleaned up and strung together, and so at last the guide.

Allan Austin, 1966

1966-72

The years during which the last guide book was written was a period of intense activity involving virtually every crag in the area. There was then a period of comparative quiet, until in 1969, Jim Fullalove climbed the right-hand arête of Stony Buttress. This climb, The Hobbit, proved to be a major route, and an event of importance, since it marked the discovery of a buttress previously overlooked by the local experts and, without a doubt, the most serious crag in the valley. Two years later, Rod Valentine added his magnificent crack climb The Ragman's Trumpet, which was followed shortly by P. Livesey's Sally Free and Easy. These routes, together with Austin's attractive 'eliminate'-type extreme, The Bracken-clock, have advanced the development of Pavey Ark to such a pitch that it is now, without doubt, the major crag in the valley.

In White Ghyll, most of the obvious gaps have now been filled, two of them giving very hard pitches indeed: Paladin was led by R. Matheson, and the roof-crack above Haste Not was led by Austin to complete, at last, the true Haste Not Direct.

On the Neckband Crag, Gillette led by K. Wood completed a fine triptych. On Gimmer there has been little activity, although Carpetbagger is a worthy addition to the excellent routes on the north-west face.

As time goes by, it has become obvious that the average new route in Langdale is shorter than its predecessor, and it is unlikely that many more big classic lines will be discovered in the valley. What is certain, however, is that climbers of the future will continue to find untrodden places to exercise their talents, and that much that is good remains to be discovered.

Allan Austin, November 1972

1972-79

The most significant developments in climbing in Langdale during the seventies can be summarised very briefly. Namely, the confirmation of Pavey Ark as the major crag of the area, the intensive development of Deer Bield Crag and that part of Gimmer Crag between The Crack and 'D' Route, and perhaps most important of all, the acceptance of a strict code of ethics by most of those climbers active in the discovery of new routes.

The publication of the last edition of this guide was clouded in controversy concerning the decision to omit certain climbs. "It is no solution at all to fail, and then go round to the top and abseil down to place a fixed piton and hanging sling, which can be reached from below, in order to by-pass a particularly troublesome spot." This stand taken by Allan Austin and Rod Valentine, over the routes Peccadillo, The Graduate, Cruel Sister and Fine Time, received a considerable amount of criticism. Developments in Langdale and elsewhere have vindicated their position; in fact, climbing ethics have advanced to the point where the use of any sort of aid, pre-placed or otherwise is rejected by many of the best climbers. Moreover, almost every aid point in Langdale, including those infamous pre-placed slings, has been eliminated.

Much of the credit for this must go to Pete Botterill and Jeff Lamb, whose efforts have elevated these controversial climbs to a position of respectability.

If the explorations of Austin had established Pavey Ark as the single most important climbing area in the Valley, then the activities of Ed Grindley indicated the potential of the crag for big, hard climbs in the modern idiom. Grindley's determined approach produced a fine trio of routes on the East Wall, climbed without prior inspection and with the use of only minimal aid. Although Fallen Angel, in its free form, is quite definitely the best of Grindley's routes, his boldest effort was the ascent of Brain Damage, over two days. So sensitive was he to the threat of another party stealing the route, that he arranged for his second to be on guard at the foot of the route at six in the morning! Since then, still harder routes have been added to Pavey's repertoire, contributions being made by most of the Valley's activists: Martin Berzins, Ed Cleasby, Ron Fawcett, Jeff Lamb and Pete Whillance, each responsible for at least one major route.

Austin's very enjoyable Whit's End Direct marked the end of his explorations in Langdale; strangely, this was the first major new route on Gimmer for almost ten years and it heralded a phase of intensive development of this part of the crag. With the exception of Pete Livesey's Eastern Hammer, the routes of this period are not major lines, but they do give most enjoyable climbing on perfect rock and in superb settings.

A surprise to many has been the emergence of Deer Bield as a major crag; although only small, Deer Bield is packed with features, especially grooves and ribs, but also a number of very steep walls.

Pete Long pointed the way when he cast Pearls Before Swine, a bold and very fine effort; but it was left to Pete Whillance and Dave Armstrong to realise the true potential of the crag with the ascents of no less than five major routes, culminating in Take it to the Limit, the most serious lead in the area. Such is the pace of modern climbing, that this route received its second ascent within two hours of the first!

The other crags in the Valley have also received detailed scrutiny, but have not yielded more than a handful of really worthwhile routes. Cleasby has been particularly active; his best route, probably, being Warrior in White Ghyll, whilst the Berzins brothers have been busy eliminating aid and adding some new routes to Flat Crags, Bowfell. However, one of the best routes of recent years is to be found on the crag beloved by those whose climbing is regulated by the licensing hours; Lamb's modern version of the aid-route Trilogy gives high quality, high standard climbing, within 10 minutes easy walk of the Old Hotel.

What for the future then? Opportunities for good new climbs now seem to be drying up—'though never let it be said that there is no room'. Certainly, there are still a few last great problems, not to mention a few esoteric corners of Langdale still awaiting development, but it is doubtful whether there are any really superb climbs awaiting discovery. Several recent climbs are eliminates or variants, very closely tied to existing routes and previously unclimbed only because they were considered unworthy of attention; no doubt, many more such routes will be "discovered". It is not easy to be optimistic about future development, but Langdale is such a superb place to climb that it will continue to be popular with all climbers, whether they are searching for new ways, or just content to follow familiar and well-blazoned trails.

M.G.M. 1980

GIMMER CRAG (277070)

The Stickle Barn Car Park and the Old Dungeon Ghyll Hotel are the usual starting points.

From behind Stickle Barn the ordinary Langdale Pikes' track leads on to the fellside, turns left and rises up the steep grass bank running north-west, above the left bank of Dungeon Ghyll. After a few hundred feet, the track zigzags over steeper ground to arrive at a large undulating plateau, with Harrison Stickle rising ahead. The track, now almost level, is still followed to the left, but, when it begins to rise again steeply to the col above where Gimmer Crag comes in sight, it is forsaken for an indefinite level trod, which keeps left over a subsidiary ridge and leads over the scree, in a few hundred yards, to the foot of South-east Gully.

From the back of the Old Hotel, the route starts up a grassy bank with fell walls on either side, turns behind the wall on the left, crosses the scree and rises, zigzagging generally in a north-westerly direction. It then keeps fairly low to avoid the deeper gullies and steeper outcrops hereabouts. Gimmer Crag, though, is soon sighted above and the track rises gradually, passing below what is in summer a very welcome little waterfall, crosses the scree and reaches again the foot of South-east Gully.

The ascent of Middlefell Buttress is a third common method of approach to Gimmer Crag. From the top of this a steep direct ascent of the fellside soon leads to the Pikes' track coming up from Stickle Barn, and this is followed as before.

Gimmer Crag, though not a Pike itself, is from the rock-climbing point of view the central attraction of the justly famous Langdale Pikes.

Seen from across the valley, the crag breaks out from the scree abruptly, almost from a single point, and rises in a gradually widening (but broken) incline, for some two hundred and fifty feet to its point of greatest width, where its form changes. Here comes a series of rounded grassy terraces. The crag's broken nature ends. It steepens and rises as a smooth, rather conical pillar for two hundred feet to a rounded top lying against the fellside.

Being but a single buttress, unmarred by gullies, its topography is simple. In general, it faces South-west but on closer inspection the rough conical shape of its upper section divides itself into three main Faces, namely, the North-west, the West, and the South-east. The North-west and the South-east Faces sweep down into the two similarly named embracing gullies which hold Gimmer Crag aloof from the general fellside. The West Face abuts on the rounded terraces forming the top of the lower broken section.

South-east Gully and Junipall Gully, situated on opposite sides of the crag, are evidence of a fault which just fails to isolate Gimmer Crag from the main mountain. Junipall Gully runs steeply down and at right angles into the North-west Gully.

The wall above Junipall Gully is known as Pallid Buttress, while the bounding wall to the South-east Gully is called Main Wall.

Approaching by the track from Great Langdale, the silhouette of the West Face and the frontal view of the South-west Face form a memorable picture. The climber arrives at the foot of South-east Gully, above the broken lower sweep of the crag; the South-east Face climbs are immediately at hand. Ahead lies the Bilberry Chute, the eastern end of one of the lower of the rounded terraces. An obvious scrambling zigzag track leads up to it and from terrace to terrace until the highest, Ash-tree Ledge, is reached. Here starts the network of the West Face climbs.

The North-west Face, with its cracks and overhangs so different from the other faces, is reached with slightly more trouble and in a variety of ways. From the foot of the Bilberry Chute, walk down alongside the buttress, round its toe, and up the steep grass in the lower part of North-west Gully. Alternatively, from about midway between the Bilberry Chute and Ash-tree Ledge, one obvious terrace entirely crosses the face, until a vertical twenty-five foot descent of some difficulty, where a rope may be of service, leads to the foot of Ash-tree Slabs. The third method adopted for reaching this face is the actual descent of Ash-tree Slabs from Ash-tree Ledge, which of course requires rope and the necessary skill. The North-west Face differs again from the other two main faces in that, while all their climbs lead to the summit (with the exception of Prelude), this face continues along the lower broken part of the crag, and the climbs on that section lead only to Ash-tree Ledge.

For descent after a climb, the South-east Gully will be found almost level with the top of the West Face and just a few yards away to the right. The usual method is to enter from the left and continue on this side until about half-way down, then crossing and finishing by the right side (looking in). A certain amount of care is needed on loose scree and one short scoop. This leads to the foot of the Bilberry Chute.

Junipall Gully leads conveniently from the top to the north-west side. It will be found by wandering up several terraces to the left from the top of the West Face. This gully, too, requires a little care—it is usually rather greasy and contains some loose scree. A direct descent to Ash-tree Ledge by one of the easier West Face climbs may involve some congestion with ascending parties.

The climbs on Pallid Buttress are readily accessible from the North-west Gully.

Main Wall Climb   160 feet   Very difficult
The right bounding wall of South-east Gully can be climbed by a variety of routes, but the most continuous and obvious is the direct route up the right hand edge. Start at an embedded rock at the foot of the wall, a little below the prominent detached flake.
1 55 feet. Climb straight up the steep wall on good holds to a ledge with an assortment of small belays.
2 30 feet. A diagonal traverse to the left leads to an obvious stance.
3 35 feet. Step right and proceed directly up again to a good belay.
4 40 feet. Start slightly left and then continue up, finishing on the left of a block, or by a scoop on its right.

Grondle Grooves   160 feet   Severe (hard)
Harder and less well-used than Main Wall. Start at the prominent flake.
1 35 feet. Climb the steep thin crack up the right side of the flake or the easy chimney on the left.
2 55 feet. Go up a short wall for a few feet; then move left to a crack slanting up to the left. Follow this until it ends in a whitish groove. Belay on a ledge just above.
3 70 feet. Climb to another ledge 20 feet higher before traversing round a blunt rib on the left. Continue up and left to a short steep wall, which leads to the top.

South-east Face

South-east Gully Only an easy scramble, providing a useful means of descent from the summit to the climbs on the South-east Face, or to the foot of the Bilberry Chute.

Bachelor Crack 175 feet Severe (hard)
The route follows the right edge of the South-east Face. Although quite exposed towards the top, the main difficulty is in the first pitch. Start from the South-east Gully at the highest accessible point, on the left wall at a corner-crack.
1 55 feet. Ascend the corner to a small ledge (junction with Chimney Buttress, which goes up to the left). Surmount the bulge and then make a delicate traverse to the rib overlooking the gully. Belay a few feet higher on a small ledge.
2 120 feet. Climb the pleasant walls and slabs to the top, passing several bilberry ledges on the way.

Chimney Buttress 210 feet Severe
The chief interest is in the long second pitch. Start in South-east Gully, a few feet below the start of Bachelor Crack.
1 40 feet. Climb a short crack and then scramble up and left to a large ledge a few feet right of Gimmer Chimney.
2 90 feet. Go diagonally right to a big block near the edge of South-east Gully (junction with Bachelor Crack). From the block ascend the steep wall above and continue up slabs to a good ledge
3 80 feet. The slabs above lead pleasantly to the top.

**Gimmer Chimney 260 feet Very difficult
A fine feature giving a good classic climb, suitable for wet weather. Start at a cairn at the foot of a broken rib.
1 100 feet. Follow the rib and the easy chimney above to a ledge below a steep section. Climb this, awkwardly, to reach easy rocks, which lead to a good stance on the right.
2 55 feet. Traverse left for 10 feet into a difficult groove, which leads to a sentry box. Climb the deep crack above, using big holds on the right rib, to a stance at the right end of the Gangway.
3 35 feet. The chimney above is part of Bracket and Slab Climb. Walk 15 feet to the right and climb the easier chimney there to the open gully above.
4 70 feet. Climb first the gully bed and then the right rib, to the summit.

***Bracket and Slab Climb** 315 feet Severe (hard)

The strenuous chimney can be avoided, in which case the grade is Severe. A long and varied climb, with considerable charm and character. Start at a pointed flake, about 20 feet above the level of the point at which the path reaches the crag.

1 35 feet. Climb over the tip of the flake to a ledge, then over an awkward slab to another ledge.

2 65 feet. Move a few feet right to the rib, which leads in 35 feet to a grassy bank. This is followed to a good ledge.

3 40 feet. The Bracket. A horizontal traverse to the right for 20 feet over large flakes is followed by a difficult groove.

4 65 feet. Traverse diagonally right over easy rocks, passing Amen Corner on the left, to reach the start of the "Neat Bit". Follow the ledge running diagonally left for 15 feet and then climb the crack to the Gangway.

5 20 feet. Walk 20 feet right to the foot of the first of two chimneys.

6 25 feet. Climb the strenuous chimney, which requires considerable effort and perseverance. It can be avoided by the much easier chimney on the right.

7 65 feet. Climb the left wall, working leftwards to a good ledge, when it is possible to move right to the edge of Gimmer Chimney. Finish straight up the slabs above.

Variation. A clean slab, right of the ordinary start, gives an entertaining pitch. Start a few yards up the gully.

1a. 50 feet. Climb the crack in the slab passing an overlap at 30 feet.

South-east Lower Traverse 95 feet Difficult

This serves as a short cut from the South-east Gully to the West face or as a useful means of descent. Start at a little cave some 50 feet above the foot of the Gully.

1 55 feet. From the small cave, follow a fault running upwards to the left to a small sentry box.

2 40 feet. Climb out over the left wall and traverse left to the foot of Amen Corner.

A higher and easier traverse leads from the start of Chimney Buttress across Gimmer Chimney, then via the slabs to the Gangway at the top of Amen Corner.

The West Face

Prelude   245 feet   Difficult
The broken rocks below Ash-tree Ledge give an uninteresting climb, the difficulties of which can be avoided at most points. Start at the lowest point of the buttress at a small ash below a sweep of slabs.
1 45 feet. Climb the slab to a spike belay.
2 65 feet. Step round to the left and go up to a groove. Continue up this and the easy rocks above to the foot of a rib.
3 55 feet. Scramble up the rib to a large flake.
4 80 feet. A short slab, a traverse left, and another slab lead to easy ground below the main face.

Crow's Nest Direct   210 feet   Very severe
An interesting climb, though rather contrived. Start at the lower right hand end of Ash-tree Ledge below a large obvious niche. The Bracket, on Bracket and Slab Climb, is 20 feet above on the right.
1 45 feet (4c). Climb the crack easily to the foot of the open groove in the left wall of the corner. Enter the groove with difficulty and follow it to a ledge.
2 55 feet (4b). Ascend the bulging wall above the small pedestal to the foot of a thin crack, 15 feet left of Amen Corner. Climb the crack to the Gangway and follow this leftwards to a small belay below an overhang.
3 60 feet (4c). Make a sensational upward hand-traverse on good holds, across the overhanging wall on the right, until a pull-out can be made onto a small ledge above the overhang. Alternatively, climb a thin steep crack above the hand-traverse. Move back leftwards to the arête right of Green Chimney, which leads to the Crow's Nest.
4 50 feet (4a). Step out to the left and climb the corner immediately above, when easy slabs lead to the summit.

Variation Start   **Green Gambit**
An easier alternative to pitch 1. Start 25 feet left of the normal start.
1a 45 feet (4b). Go up easy rocks and climb the green overhanging groove to an awkward exit.

**'B' Route 170 feet Severe (mild)

Justifiably popular. Towards the end of Ash Tree Ledge, where it slopes down to the right, a large platform can be seen up on the right. Start by scrambling up to this platform.

1 35 feet. Climb a short crack on the right to reach Thomson's Ledge. Go 20 feet to the right to the foot of Amen Corner.
2 15 feet. Climb the impending corner to reach the Gangway.
3 30 feet. Ascend the Gangway to the left to a good ledge.
4 40 feet. Climb Green Chimney, immediately above, until a short traverse to the right gives access to a comfortable ledge, the Crow's Nest.
5 50 feet. Step right and follow pleasant slabs to the top.

*'C' Route 170 feet Severe

A pleasing and fairly direct route up the face. Start by scrambling up to the large platform, as for 'B' Route.

1 70 feet. Climb the steep wall and pull awkwardly into a steep scoop which leads to Thomson's Ledge. Move right to a flake at the foot of a steep groove (possible belay). Climb the right side of the flake to reach the groove and follow this until it is possible to step right to a belay at the foot of Green Chimney.
2 100 feet. Move left, and then climb diagonally left (across Lyons Crawl) under the obvious square-cut overhang, to reach a ledge level with the overhang. Or, perhaps more interesting, climb the left edge of Green Chimney and traverse horizontally left under the overhang. Step up and right and climb directly up (steep and exposed) to the finishing balcony.

**'A' Route 185 feet Severe (mild)

A series of steps rising to the left from Thomson's Ledge. Start by scrambling up to the platform as for 'B' and 'C' Routes.

1 15 feet. Climb the initial crack of 'B' route to a belay on Thomson's Ledge.
2 30 feet. Traverse left along Thomson's Ledge to the foot of the 'Forty-foot Corner'.
3 60 feet. Climb the corner to a good spike at the top and traverse left to below an open groove (Lichen Chimney).
4 35 feet. Climb Lichen Chimney. Good flake belay on the wall 6 feet above and to the left of the finish.
5 45 feet. Follow the rock staircase on the left to a crack, which leads to the top.

Dipthong (140 feet Severe (hard)) gives a direct way up the crag but is very artificial. The climb starts up the obvious break above the platform, left of the start of 'C' Route. The right edge of the Forty-foot Corner is followed and then a line just right of 'C' Route.

**Oliverson's Variation and Lyon's Crawl 150 feet Very difficult
The easiest line up this part of the crag; gives varied and interesting
climbing. Start from Ash-tree Ledge, 15 feet to the left of the
start of 'A' and 'B' routes and scramble up to a good belay.

1 50 feet. Traverse horizontally right on good holds for 15 feet
and then go directly up the left edge of the Forty Foot Corner
to its top.

2 50 feet. Lyons Crawl. Traverse upwards and to the right along
an obvious crack to a large ledge. Continue up to the right
into Green Chimney and then across the right wall into the
Crow's Nest.

3 50 feet. Step right and follow pleasant slabs to the top (as for
'B' Route).

'E' Route 210 feet Severe (hard)
Delicate and somewhat exposed. Start by scrambling up to the
platform as for 'A', 'B' and 'C' Routes.

1 25 feet. Climb a little overhanging corner on the left to easy
rocks and a stance.

2 55 feet. Traverse the flaky wall diagonally left for 40 feet to a
ledge and move across to belay on the right rib of a crack.

3 30 feet. Climb the crack for 15 feet, when a delicate traverse
can be made to the right to the foot of Lichen Chimney.

4 85 feet. Continue the traverse upwards, crossing the blunt
arête to reach a small ledge. Go back left a few feet, round the
arête to a groove and climb up to a ledge which runs from
'C' Route to the top of Lichen Chimney. Continue up the steep
wall in front to the finishing balcony, roughly midway between
'A' and 'C' Routes.

Lichen Groove 160 feet Severe (hard)
A direct line by way of the shallow groove, which becomes most
pronounced as Lichen Chimney. Start on Ash Tree Ledge, just
to the left of 'A' and 'B' Routes at the foot of a slight nose.

1 30 feet. Climb the thin crack in the right edge of the nose to
belay on 'E' Route.

2 60 feet. Step up and right, and move up the wall awkwardly,
into a shallow groove. Follow the groove up to the left on
small holds to the foot of Lichen Chimney.

3 70 feet. Climb Lichen Chimney, or the ill defined groove
just on the right. Finish up the corner above on good holds.

**'D' Route   100 feet   Severe

A route of considerable character. Start about 40 feet above Ash-tree Ledge at a terrace below a triangular recess, reached by scrambling up to the left from a point 20 feet to the left of Oliverson's Traverse.

1 100 feet. Climb up to and into the recess; traverse delicately left for 15 feet and follow the groove and crack line to the top.

Musgrave's Traverse   140 feet   Severe (hard)

The most obvious and direct connection between the end of South-east Lower Traverse and 'D' Route. Start from Thomson's Ledge at a crack a few feet left of Amen Corner.

1 55 feet. Climb the narrow crack to a sloping ledge on the right and then follow a three-inch ledge up to the left for 20 feet to an airy right-angled corner, from which a delicate descending traverse can be made into the groove of 'C' Route. Go up this for a few feet and continue to the foot of Green Chimney.

2 40 feet. Traverse delicately leftwards, past the top of the Forty-foot Corner and move up a little to the foot of Lichen Chimney.

3 45 feet. Make a delicate horizontal traverse left to 'D' Route. The descent of Hyphen is the most appropriate finish.

Hyphen   90 feet   Severe

A pleasant traverse, useful as a connection between Asterisk and 'D' Route, thus making quite a long, continuous climb. Start from the terrace above the left end of Ash-tree Ledge.

1 90 feet. Climb up to a small ledge beneath the overhang and traverse diagonally right to a narrow ledge leading to a bulging corner. Step delicately round the corner to join 'D' Route.

*Spring Bank   140 feet   Extremely severe (E1)

An exceedingly pleasant eliminate, with an exhilarating overhang. Start just left of 'D' Route.

1 140 feet (5b). Follow the rib, just left of 'D' Route and continue up thin cracks to the centre of the roof. Pull over this and finish directly up the slab.

Whit's End 165 feet Very severe

A hybrid route, which provides both strenuous and delicate climbing of considerable interest. Start a few feet left of 'D' Route at the foot of a thin crack.

1 45 feet (4c). Climb the crack and ascend diagonally left by means of a good flake to a small stance beneath the overhang.

2 50 feet (4c). Follow the corner above ('F' Route) for 15 feet, until it is possible to make a delicate traverse across the steep slab. Continue the traverse along small ledges to an awkward step down into 'D' Route. Belay a few feet higher.

4 70 feet (4c). Ascend 'D' Route for a few feet to a very thin horizontal crack on the left. Swing out left along this and pull up into a scoop. Step across the left wall of the scoop and make an intimidating move onto the front, where the difficulties ease and big holds lead pleasantly to the top.

*Whit's End Direct 140 feet Extremely severe (E1)

Another enjoyable eliminate, through the barrier of overhangs left of 'D' Route. Start at the foot of the thin crack of Whit's End.

1 140 feet (5b). Climb the crack and continue up a line of thin cracks to the step in the left end of the overhangs. Make a sensational move right, onto the slab, and finish pleasantly on good small holds.

**'F' Route 120 feet Very severe

The obvious corner crack gives a classic climb of great character; the line is clean and direct, with the crux where it should be: right at the top. Start a few feet left of Whit's End by scrambling up to a ledge a little way up Hyphen.

1 120 feet (4c). Move across to the right to a small ledge above the thin crack of Whit's End; then climb diagonally left by means of a good flake to a small ledge beneath the overhangs. Step up right, into the corner, and follow it to a bold and strenuous finish.

*Poacher 125 feet Very severe (hard)

The slim groove, left of the upper part of 'F' Route, provides exposed and enjoyable climbing. Start as for 'F' Route.

1 85 feet (5a). Follow 'F' Route to a niche at the foot of the corner proper. Climb up to the little roof and make a bold move left onto the face. Step up, and then move diagonally left to a good spike at the foot of the slim groove. Go up this to the best stance on Gimmer.

2 40 feet (4c). Finish up the groove directly above the ledge.

Poacher Right Hand 120 feet Extremely severe (E1)
Technically interesting but rather close to 'F' Route.
1 120 feet (5b). Follow 'F' Route to the niche of Poacher. Pull
straight over the roof and make a couple of exciting moves up
the rib to the right end of the Poacher belay ledge. Continue
up the wall above with some difficulty.

Enormous Room 120 feet Extremely severe (E3)
A few, very difficult moves and good positions. Start as for 'F'
Route and Poacher.
1 120 feet (6a). Follow Poacher to the good spike, move down
and make a long reach into Eastern Hammer. Continue left
to a junction with Kipling Groove, move left again and
finish up a groove.

**Eastern Hammer 130 feet Extremely severe (E3)
Steep and fingery climbing through the bulges left of Poacher.
Start from the ledge at the foot of 'F' Route.
1 130 feet (6a). Pull over the overhang and follow the crack to a
good hold below the final bulges. Step up on this and cross
the bulge on the left, stepping immediately back right to a
ledge. Finish easily up the final cracks of Kipling Groove.

*Equus 140 feet Extremely severe (E2)
The slim groove between Kipling Groove and Eastern Hammer.
Start from the ledge at the foot of 'F' Route.
1 140 feet (5b). Move up and left and pull over the roof at its
mid-point to reach the groove, with some difficulty. Continue
up this more easily until forced left onto Kipling Groove and
go up to the resting place below the crux. Swing left to a small
ledge, climb a groove and the face on the right (very exposed)
to reach a horizontal crack. Follow this left to finish.

***Kipling Groove 135 feet Very severe (hard)
A superb and strenuous way up an impressive piece of rock;
classic and justly popular. Start from the ledge at the foot of 'F'
Route.
1 35 feet (4c). Move up and traverse under the overhang to a
crack which leads to an overhung recess.
2 100 feet (5a). Climb the right wall of the recess to the overhang,
step right onto the edge and follow a crack to a resting place
below the bulge. Pull across strenuously to a diagonal crack
(crux) and climb up to a horizontal crack. Traverse right to a
small ledge, where a crack leads to easier ground and the
top.

Variation Finish
Move left above the diagonal crack and go up to a narrow ledge at the foot of a smooth little groove. Either climb this (very awkward) or slightly easier, step round the corner on the left and climb a little wall. Both ways are harder than the usual finish.

Barry's Traverse 75 feet Very severe (mild)
The easiest direct link between Ash-tree Ledge and The Crack and Hiatus; useful as a continuation of the West Face traverses. Start at the extreme left-hand end of Ash-tree Ledge.
1 40 feet (4b). Climb leftwards over easy grass and rocks until a short, steep descent leads to a ledge on the right wall of the 'unclimbed section' of The Crack.
2 35 feet (4c). Make a delicate descending traverse into the corner when a strenuous pull-up leads to a ledge on the left wall. Follow the ledge to the pedestal belay of The Crack. Hiatus is just to the left.

North-west Face (Lower Section)

Interlude 90 feet Very difficult
Start about 40 feet below a large detached flake in the lower reaches of North-west Gully.
1 90 feet. Climb the right wall of an arête and make an awkward step left onto the arête itself. Follow easy slabs to broken ground.

Cartwheel (70 feet Very difficult) follows a line parallel with Interlude, starting from a small boulder about 25 feet below the large flake.

Herdwick Buttress 90 feet Very difficult
Start just to the right of the foot of Ash-tree Slabs.
1 40 feet. Ascend the open chimney on the right to a large ledge.
2 50 feet. Climb up between two large flakes to twin cracks, which lead to the terrace below 'D' Route.

Introduction (75 feet Severe (hard)) follows the left edge of the steep slab to the left of Herdwick Buttress, the hardest part being near the top. Start from the small bay below Ash-tree Slabs.

*Ash-tree Slabs   155 feet   Very difficult
Some distance above the detached flake, there is an extensive
sweep of slabs, left of a prominent leaning corner. Start from a
small bay at the foot of the corner.
1 50 feet. Move 10 feet up the corner, traverse diagonally left on
  good holds to the edge and follow this to a ledge.
2 105 feet. Climb to a platform below a groove leading up to the
  right; follow this and the slabs above to the terrace below the
  West Face.

Joas   150 feet   Very severe
Strenuous but rather contrived. Start from a platform 20 feet
left of Ash-tree Slabs.
1 30 feet (4c). Ascend the overhanging groove to a broken
  terrace.
2 40 feet (4c). Climb the overhanging block by the crack on its
  right to a small recess, move left on a good flake and pull over
  the overhang to a small ledge. Continue slightly left until a
  long step across to the right can be made to a thin crack,
  which leads with difficulty to the platform on pitch 2 of Ash-
  tree Slabs.
3 80 feet (4c). Follow the narrow slab on the left, then climb
  a corner and finish up the arête on the right.

* Intern   155 feet   Very severe (hard)
Varied and sustained climbing. Start up Joas.
1 60 feet (5b). Follow Joas for about 10 feet, and cross the
  slab which slants up to the left and narrows towards the top
  left hand corner. Go up on the left edge; overlooking the
  gully, until a pull can be made into a short groove. Climb it
  to the foot of a leftward slanting gangway.
2 95 feet (5a). Go up the gangway for a few feet before stepping
  right to climb the wall above the belay. Pull over the bulge,
  boldly, to reach a steep groove. Follow this to a rib, which
  leads to the steep final crack of North-west Arête.

North-west Arête   135 feet   Very severe (mild)
The arête left of Intern gives exposed and satisfying climbing
on good holds. Start below a large overhang to the left of the
arête, a few feet right of Asterisk.
1 135 feet (4b). Climb the wall and traverse to the right to below
  a groove, left of the overhang. Follow the groove, and traverse
  right immediately above the overhang to the arête, which can
  be climbed more or less direct to finish via a thin crack.

**Asterisk 125 feet Severe (hard)

A popular climb up the steep wall on the left of North-west Arête. Start to the right of the large jammed boulder in the bed of the gully.

1 125 feet. Follow the easiest line up the left side of the wall for about 60 feet to a narrow ledge; then make a horizontal traverse right to the ridge. Ascend diagonally left to a thin crack which leads to the top, with some difficulty. Alternatively, climb the wall just left of the crack. It is possible to avoid this final section by escaping rightwards.

Samaritan Corner 130 feet Severe (hard)

A companion route to Asterisk, but slightly easier, following the obvious corner on its left. Start at the foot of the corner.

1 130 feet. Follow the corner, more or less direct, for about 70 feet; finish up the right wall.

Breaking Point 240 feet Extremely severe (E2)

Very much an eliminate climb, but nevertheless worthwhile. Start at the foot of The Crack.

1 80 feet (5a). Climb the slab on the right until the wall steepens. Step up and left, then climb up right to gain a crack. Follow this to easier ground and belay about 20 feet below the obvious, wide crack on Gimmer String.

2 80 feet (5c). Go up to the foot of the wide crack and step down left onto the large spike. Make a long reach and pull over the roof; move left strenuously to reach a groove and follow it to a good ledge on The Crack ('The Bower').

3 80 feet (5c). Climb the wall above The Bower and step right to a junction with Gimmer String. Go up the steep little groove (Gimmer String escapes left from this onto the rib) and move right to finish up another steep groove (Equus uses this groove but moves out right).

**Gimmer String 250 feet Extremely severe (E1)

Follows a line, more or less directly, from The Crack to the stance on Kipling Groove, before moving out onto the great undercut arête between the front of Gimmer and The Crack. The climb is attractively laid out with its major difficulties in fine open situations on the arête, and gives one of the most enjoyable routes on Gimmer.

1 85 feet (4b). Follow the first pitch of The Crack.

2 85 feet (4c). Cross easily to the right to the top of a pinnacle below the large overhang and step right to below a wide

crack. Pull awkwardly into the crack and follow it to the stance on Kipling Groove.

3 80 feet (5b). Climb directly up for a few feet to some large blocks; then traverse across to a small undercut and overhung ledge on the rib. Go up a thin crack on the right hand side of the arête, until it is possible to pull round, with difficulty, onto the other side overlooking The Crack. Climb the arête, trending left up a thin crack, until forced out right onto the wall with an abrupt finish on a good ledge. The top lies just above.

***The Crack   240 feet   Very severe

The best line in the valley and the classic crack climb of the Lake District. Varied climbing and a reasonable standard that is maintained throughout, contribute to a superb outing. Start at the foot of an easy-angled groove, which soon merges into the crack proper.

1 85 feet (4b). Scramble up the groove and follow the crack until it is possible to traverse left to the foot of a short groove. Climb the groove to a ledge and pedestal belay. (A strenuous alternative to the traverse is to continue up the crack for 10 feet before moving left to the pedestal).

2 85 feet (4c). Ascend thin cracks above the belay, moving left and up to a large ledge at 25 feet. Continue up the steep little ridge and traverse easily back right into the crack. Follow this to a superb ledge (The Bower), which is attained after a strenuous pull-up.

3 70 feet (4b). Climb the crack direct to the finish.

Gimmer High Girdle   190 feet   Extremely severe (E1)

A high level traverse from The Crack to Whit's End. An enjoyable climb with sustained exposure. Start from The Bower.

1 110 feet (5a). Climb the wall above The Bower and step right to a junction with Gimmer String. Follow this up the thin crack and the arête, until it is possible to step right to a small ledge. Make a very exposed swing right and go down to the good resting place on Kipling Groove. Pull across, strenuously, to a diagonal crack (crux of Kipling Groove). Climb this and continue to the right along a break until it is possible to step down onto the stance of Poacher.

2 80 feet (5b). Traverse right and swing into 'F' Route. Continue right to join Whit's End Direct. Step out right above the overhang and traverse right along the lip to join Whit's End; finish up this.

Dight 230 feet Extremely severe (E1)
An interesting climb up the wall left of The Crack. Start at the foot of The Crack.

1 70 feet (5b). Go up The Crack to a crack which bends left to the right-hand of two grooves. Climb this to the first stance of The Crack.

2 110 feet (5a). Follow The Crack for about 40 feet to the top of the short rib. Trend easily rightwards to a ledge below the overlaps. Make a hard pull over the left-hand end of the overhang into the thin crack above. Follow the crack to cross a second and smaller overhang and go up more easily to a sentry-box on the left. Ascend the crack on the left to more overhangs and move right to a small stance.

3 50 feet (5a). Climb the corner above the stance for a few feet before pulling up strenuously, round a small rib, into the groove on the right. Climb this to easier ground and the top.

Variations

1a 70 feet (4c). The groove left of pitch 1.

2a 100 feet (5c). It is possible to vary pitch 2 by leaving the crack earlier to climb a thin crack on the right and then following a more direct line to the stance. Very artificial.

3a 50 feet (5b). Step out right onto the wall and go direct to the top.

*Hiatus 325 feet Very severe
The climb follows the vegetated sweep of slabs to the left of The Crack and turns the prominent overhangs on the left by a long and exposed traverse. The turning of the overhangs provides a magnificent finish, an adequate reward for a somewhat indifferent start. Start a few feet to the left of the foot of The Crack.

1 105 feet. Follow the easy slabs to a ledge in the corner on the right below a grassy gully.

2 105 feet. Ascend the gully for 30 feet until it is possible to move left along a ledge and then go back right into the gully along another ledge. After a few feet traverse left across a mossy wall to some ledges.

3 70 feet (4b). Go up into the corner under the overhang; then step across a large block and follow a rising traverse left, below the overhangs, to a steep corner. Climb this for 10 feet; step left, first up, then down, and continue the traverse under an overhanging rib to a second rib. Ascend this to a fine niche.

4 45 feet (4b). Climb the slab on the left and a short awkward scoop leading to easy scrambling.

Bridges Variation

3a 70 feet (4c). From the steep corner climb up and over the rib to the niche.

4a 40 feet (4c). Climb the steep, black-looking chimney.

Inertia 165 feet Very severe (hard)
The slabs left of Dight are approached via a steep groove in the bounding rib of Hiatus. Start from a ledge on pitch 2 of Hiatus, below the groove.

1 90 feet (5a). Go up the groove to the top of a small pedestal in the corner and pull round the overhang into the groove on the right. Ascend this for a few feet and traverse out to the rib on the right; make a hard move up the rib, and go up and across to the Dight sentry box. Climb the crack on the left and step right to the small stance.

2 75 feet (5a). Climb the long narrow slab and, where it steepens, the corner-crack to the end of a line of small square-cut overhangs (junction with Grooves Traverse); then go up to the right to the top.

*Grooves Superdirect 130 feet Very severe (hard)
Technically interesting and exposed. Start from a ledge on pitch 2 of Hiatus, about 90 feet above the stance and below and to the left of an obvious overhang.

1 75 feet (5a). Go up to the overhang (above and left of the groove on Inertia) and move right under it until some strenuous pulls lead to the edge of the slab overlooking Dight. Trend up and left to the stance on Grooves Traverse.

2 55 feet (5b). Climb the scoop for 20 feet until an awkward move leads into the shallow groove on the left. Step left again and ascend rightwards to rejoin the main groove, just below the top.

Variation

2a 50 feet (5b). Climb the groove direct.

*Grooves Traverse 110 feet Very severe (hard)
A harder finish to Hiatus and more exposed. The overhangs are turned by a long traverse to the right. Start from the stance below pitch 3 of Hiatus.

1 55 feet (4c). Follow pitch 3 to the level of the large block. Make a strenuous traverse right across the steep wall into a groove, which leads to a small stance below a scoop.

2 55 feet (5a). Climb the scoop for 10 feet and then make a very delicate traverse right beneath a small overhang. Continue rightwards up a slanting groove which leads to the top.

Carpetbagger 245 feet Very severe
A companion route to Hiatus but a little more difficult. Start at a little slab below the right hand rib of Godiva Groove.
1 90 feet (4b). Ascend the little slab to a ledge at 20 feet; go up the shallow groove and continue on the right of the rib for 30 feet to another ledge. Traverse horizontally to the right, underneath a doubtful flake, to a stance below a large overhang.
2 90 feet (4b). Move out left, and make a long ascending traverse to the left below some overhangs. Just before reaching the rib of Godiva Groove, pull up onto a little slab and climb an awkward groove to the stance at the end of pitch 3 of Hiatus.
3 65 feet (4b). Make a short traverse right, pull up, and continue more easily to the top.

Godiva Groove 185 feet Very severe (mild)
A more or less direct line up the obvious V-groove left of Hiatus. Start by scrambling out of North-west Gully to a ledge below the left-bounding rib of the groove.
1 30 feet. Make a rising traverse to the right into the groove, which leads to a stance.
2 75 feet (4b). Ascend the groove, with excursions onto the left rib when necessary.
3 80 feet (4b). Continue up the groove for a few feet, then move onto the left wall and climb direct to the overhang. Go left into another groove and finish up the steep but broken wall above. (An alternative finish is to climb the clean rib on the right and move right to the final stance on Hiatus.)

Juniper Buttress 190 feet Severe (mild)
A pleasant climb on the right bounding wall of Junipall Gully. Start by scrambling out to the right a little above the bottom of the gully to a ledge just below, and to the right of, a small ash.
1 45 feet. Follow the rib immediately to the right of the ash to a large flake belay in a gully on the left.
2 50 feet. Traverse horizontally right for 30 feet to a corner under a nose. Climb over the nose into a V-groove; ascend this until good holds on the rib lead to a small stance.
3 55 feet. Continue up the rib and make a traverse left, first across a gully, along ledges and then across a slab. Ascend a little, step across an awkward corner and round a rib to a comfortable recess.
4 40 feet. Ascend the steep rib on the right to finish on easy ground.

Junipall Gully separates the North-west Face from Pallid Buttress and is a convenient means of descent to the north-west side of the crag.

Pallid Buttress

Nocturne   190 feet   Very severe (mild)
A pleasantly exposed route up the left wall of Junipall Gully.
Start in the gully a few feet above the lowest point of the buttress
and below a prominent line of overhangs.
1 60 feet (4b). Traverse left across a narrow slab towards a rib, to
   the point where the overhangs have almost disappeared. Pull
   over at a mossy crack and work rightwards to a good ledge.
2 90 feet (4b). Ascend directly to the overhang, turning it by a
   short traverse to the right, followed by the ascent of a shallow
   crack. When the holds become small, traverse back left and
   go up to a recess.
3 40 feet (4b). Ascend diagonally left to a small ledge on the
   arête; go up a corner and a thin crack, when easy climbing
   leads to the top.

Variations
1a 40 feet. Start higher in the gully and follow a zig-zag crack
    to the stance.
1b 110 feet. Climb a groove right of the zig-zag crack, until a
    step left leads to a junction with pitch 2.

*Pallid Slabs   185 feet   Severe
A route providing delicate climbing of considerable quality.
Start a short distance to the left of Nocturne, from the top of a
large boulder.
1 65 feet. Step onto the slabs from the boulder and make a long
   rising traverse to the right, under a series of small overhangs,
   to a good ledge (junction with Nocturne).
2 50 feet. Climb the wall on the left to a ledge on the left, the
   last few feet being particularly delicate.
3 70 feet. Step round into a groove from the left end of the ledge
   and go up past a tiny cave, heathery ledges and a corner, to
   finish up a short steep crack.

Paleface   155 feet   Severe
A climb of increasing interest with a fine finish. Start below a
shallow chimney 20 feet left of the start of Pallid Slabs.
1 75 feet. Climb more or less direct to a ledge at the top of a
   steep mossy wall.
2 80 feet. Ascend direct to the overhang and avoid it by an
   exhilarating traverse to the right, leading up to a flat ledge and
   an easy traverse back to the left. Climb the wall above on
   sloping holds to an abrupt finish.

Wall End   125 feet   Severe (mild)

The easiest of the routes on this buttress. Start at the foot of a rib forming the left end of the main Pallid Buttress.

1 95 feet. Climb the rib until forced right; keep traversing for 15 feet to a narrow ledge at the foot of a V-groove, which leads to a comfortable niche. Make a diagonal ascent to the left to a sloping ledge and go up the steep wall to a large ledge.

2 30 feet. Finish up easy slabs or a more difficult groove on the right.

Ashen Traverse   205 feet   Very severe (mild)

Girdles Pallid Buttress from right to left, finishing up a smooth slab on the subsidiary crag beyond Wall End. Start from a ledge in Junipall Gully at the top of its first chimney pitch.

1 70 feet (4c). Traverse across the wall to a large flake on the right of a conspicuous streak of black moss. Step awkwardly across the moss to the shallow crack on pitch 2 of Nocturne. Follow this for a few feet until it is possible to traverse left round a corner and across a slab to the ledge at the top of pitch 2 of Pallid Slabs.

2 30 feet. Continue the traverse across a chimney and along a ledge to a niche.

3 40 feet. Step round the corner and follow a ledge downwards to the left, past a groove, until a long stride leads round into a large recess below an imposing crack.

4 65 feet (4c). Climb the 'Crimson Crack' direct or, more pleasantly, after 15 feet go diagonally left across the wall for a few feet; then go straight up to the top.

**The Girdle Traverse   690 feet   Very severe (hard)

A magnificent expedition, traversing the whole of the main buttress from South-east Gully to Junipall Gully. The climbing is always interesting and exposed, especially so across the North-west Face. The traverse may be extended to include Pallid Buttress by means of Ashen Traverse. Start in South-east Gully at the foot of Bachelor Crack.

1 110 feet (4b). Climb the corner on Bachelor Crack and follow a horizontal traverse left to the stance above the twin chimneys (top of pitch 4, Gimmer Chimney). Continue round the corner and over easy rocks to a belay overlooking the Gangway.

2 40 feet (4c). Step down a few feet and cross the impending wall to the Gangway by a descending hand-traverse (part of pitch 3, Crow's Nest Direct, reversed). Continue up the gangway to the belay at the foot of Green Chimney.

3 95 feet (4a). Take the easiest line leftwards to the foot of

Lichen Chimney and follow Musgraves Traverse across the steep wall to 'D' Route.

4 50 feet (4a). Step down, and traverse down diagonally left to reach the stance at the start of Kipling Groove (Hyphen, reversed).

5 60 feet (5a). Traverse left under the overhang to the crack, as for Kipling Groove, and continue the traverse into a groove on the left. Climb this with difficulty to The Bower.

6 100 feet (4c). Climb The Crack for a few feet, then traverse across to the sentry box on Dight. Pull into the crack and follow it to some overhangs. Traverse left again under the overhangs and after a long stride, pull up into a groove which leads to the stance on Grooves Traverse.

7 40 feet (4c). Traverse down left to the large detached block on Hiatus (pitch 1, Grooves Traverse, reversed).

8 50 feet (4b). Go up into the corner under the overhang; then step across a large block and follow a rising traverse left below the overhangs to a steep corner. Climb this for 10 feet, step left, first up, then down and continue the traverse under an overhanging rib to a second rib. Ascend this to a fine niche (pitch 3, Hiatus).

9 105 feet (4b). Move round the corner to the left and pull across an open chimney to a traverse which leads to a junction with Juniper Buttress. Continue left to the edge (the start of Ashen Traverse lies immediately across the Gully) and finish up the rib of Juniper Buttress.

Variation

6a 85 feet (5a). Climb The Crack past the overhang to a small ledge. After a few more feet, traverse horizontally across the wall for 10 feet to a steep corner, bounded on the left by an overhung groove. Climb the corner until it is possible to work diagonally left to a stance in a broken groove (the final groove of Grooves Traverse).

7a 35 feet (5a). Step down and make a delicate traverse below a small overhang into a scoop, which leads down to a small stance (part of pitch 2, Grooves Traverse, reversed).

WHITE GHYLL (298071)

Situated in Great Langdale, White Ghyll lies parallel to Mill Ghyll, a half mile to the east. It rises steeply from a point a few hundred yards short of Stickle Barn, ill defined at first but boldly modelled near the sky-line, where the crag, towering grandly above its narrow, stony bed, presents a most striking picture as seen from the valley.

The climbs may be reached from the main road in less than half an hour. From Stickle Barn cross the stream behind the hotel and follow a rising track across the fields until the ghyll is reached. Ascending directly up the ghyll from here, a steep outcrop on the left (Swine Knott) is passed and, soon afterwards, a sycamore gained. This is the usual base for the Lower Crag, which now rises immediately on the right.

White Ghyll Crag forms the true left bank of the ghyll for a considerable distance from its summit and, for convenience of description, can be separated into an upper and a lower section, the dividing mark being some 40 yards above the prominent sycamore, where a grassy rake (the left-hand one of a pair) slants up to the right, drops a little on to a broad, grass shelf (The Great Shelf), then rises smoothly to the top; this is Easy Rake, a convenient means of descent.

The Upper Crag is split by a narrow, but imposing fissure, White Ghyll Chimney. On the left of the Chimney is a fine sweep of slabs, on the right a most aggressive-looking wall, protected at half-height by a series of formidable overhangs which hardly relent until the right-hand terminus of the wall at Easy Rake. The routes on this wall give some of the finest climbing in the district.

The Lower Crag begins, on the left, as a steep, but short, wall, topped by a secondary tier of rock, from which it is separated by the Great Shelf. It then becomes broken into a number of sharply defined grooves, many of which give short climbs of considerable quality, finally merging into the fellside at the entrance to the ghyll.

The standard of the climbs, both in difficulty and quality, is generally high; the rock is adequately cohesive, the situations often unique. The climbs are described from right to left, that is as seen when ascending the ghyll.

Lower Crag

The first feature of note is a prominent ridge, Junction Arête. On its right The Sidings offer a few short pitches of moderate difficulty reached by an unpleasantly earthy scramble up the side of the ghyll.

Junction Arête   150 feet   Severe (Difficult if the first pitch is avoided)
Two oaks in a groove on the right help to identify a route of some interest. Start at the foot of the ridge.
1 60 feet. Follow a short slab to the overhang which leads rather awkwardly to easier ground on the right. Continue up to a stance level with the first oak.
2 90 feet. Climb the ridge pleasantly to the top.

Junction Arête is bounded on the left by a broad, cracked wall. A prominent projecting nose marks the line of a short two-pitch climb. The interest is fair and the standard severe. Beyond this cracked wall there are a series of open grooves. The next two climbs start at the same point, a large block at the foot of the second groove; it is reached by scrambling up broken rocks a few yards left of Junction Arête. Both routes provide interesting climbing.

Russet Groove   90 feet   Severe
This climb rejects the V-groove above the block in favour of the similar, but less challenging fault on the right.
1 40 feet. Follow the easy slab up to the right to a stance in the groove.
2 50 feet. Climb the groove on small holds for 20 feet to a ledge on the right wall. The short, steep wall above on the left leads to the top.

Heather Groove   90 feet   Severe
The steep V-groove.
1 40 feet. Climb the overhanging corner above the block to a small ledge below a slab, which is climbed to a stance on its left edge.
2 50 feet. Return to the right hand side of the slab and climb direct to the top.

Ethics of War   80 feet   Very severe (hard)

A short but fine undercut rib, left of Heather Groove. It is possible to avoid the overhang, in which case the grade is Very severe. Start by scrambling rightwards from the foot of Laugh Not, to reach the foot of the rib.

1 80 feet (5a). Climb up rightwards under the overhang on good holds until it is possible to pull leftwards over the overhang to gain the rib. Follow this directly to the top.

Inferno   80 feet   Severe

The groove next to Heather Groove, conspicuous with its overhang at 30 feet. Broken rocks below the groove provide introductory pitches if required but it is usual to start by scrambling rightwards from the foot of Laugh Not.

1 80 feet. Climb the groove to a grass ledge on the right. Walk off to the right or climb the short groove on the left.

Not Again   80 feet   Severe

The line is closely tied to Inferno. Start at the foot of the groove of Inferno.

1 30 feet. Climb the obvious twin cracks on the right to a junction with Heather Groove below an overhang.

2 50 feet. Step left round a rib on the wall above the overhang. Make a couple of awkward moves left into a crack which is followed to a narrow ledge. Go up right to the top. Alternatively, after a few feet in the crack traverse back to the right and climb the airy rib above the stance.

Feet of Clay   80 feet   Extremely severe (E1)

A slim overhung groove in the rib separating the corners of Inferno and Laugh Not, marks the route, which has a few interesting moves. Start at the foot of Inferno.

1 80 feet (5b). Follow a short crack on the left which leads to a ledge at the foot of the groove. Climb this to the overhang where a difficult move leads right onto a steep wall. Go straight up this to a peg belay on the left.

*Man of Straw   90 feet   Extremely severe (E1)

Delightful climbing, with sustained technical interest. Start below and to the left of the slim overhung groove.

1 90 feet (5b). Climb a boot-wide crack to the ledge at the foot of the groove. Make a move or two up this, until a good hold on the left hand rib enables a short traverse to be made onto the slabby wall of Laugh Not. Go up for a few feet and then move back right delicately to the rib, which leads to a good stance and peg belay just below the top.

**Laugh Not   115 feet   Very severe (hard)
This is a fine climb, steep, clean, inescapable and challenging. It goes up the big groove to the left of Inferno, turning the overhangs by a traverse to the right. Start at a belay in the groove a few feet below the smooth section.
1 115 feet (5a). Climb the smooth corner (excellent protection) to the roof (good chockstone runner) and traverse right to the peg belay of Man of Straw.

Variation (5c). It is possible to make a very difficult rising traverse from a few feet up Laugh Not to join Man of Straw.

Waste Not, Want Not   100 feet   Extremely severe (E1)
Contrived but with interesting climbing. Start as for Laugh Not.
1 100 feet (5b). Ascend the corner for a few feet until a traverse left can be made (above Do Not). Move up to a small ledge. Climb the thin groove above, until it is possible to make a few difficult moves left to a junction with Do Not. Climb a groove directly to the top.

Do Not   115 feet   Extremely severe (E1)
Goes up the left wall of Laugh Not. The first pitch gives an awkward and unusual piece of climbing and the second pitch is fine and in an exposed situation. Start as for Laugh Not.
1 45 feet (5b). Climb up to below the smooth part of the groove, when it is possible to move onto the bulging left wall and follow a wide crack slanting up to the left to a roomy ledge (junction with Slip Knot).
2 70 feet (5a). Climb the shallow square-cut groove, above on the right, to an overhang. Traverse steeply left across the wall using a prominent flake, (as a foothold or handhold, according to choice) until a final awkward move round the nose brings good holds within reach. Continue, without further difficulty to the top.

Direct Start   80 feet   Very severe (hard)
Start below the broken-looking groove in the rib between Slip Knot and Laugh Not.
1 80 feet (5a). Climb the groove to a ledge below the overhang. Step right, round the corner and climb a steep thin crack in the wall to the stance.

Slip Knot Variations   135 feet   Extremely severe (E2)
Start below the broken-looking groove in the rib.
1 70 feet (5c). Scramble up the easy groove until it is possible to
   pull into a thin crack on the left wall. Climb this with difficulty,
   to reach a groove which leads to the big ledge.
2 65 feet (5c). Pull over the overhang and reach a groove with
   considerable difficulty. Climb this directly to join the Do Not
   traverse. Alternatively, the groove can be left low down by a
   bold traverse onto the front.

**Slip Knot   135 feet   Very severe (mild)
Immediately above the sycamore in the Ghyll is a conspicuous
right-angled corner, topped by a large triangular overhang. This
justly popular climb takes the right wall of the corner and turns
the overhang on the left. Start at the foot of the corner.
1 70 feet (4a). Climb the corner for a few feet, until excellent
   holds lead up the right wall to the good ledge.
2 65 feet (4b). Work leftwards into the corner over shattered
   rocks and make an awkward stride out to the far rib. Climb
   this, turning an overhang on the left and continue to the top.
   Belays well back.

Moss Wall   140 feet   Very severe
The next corner to the left of Slip Knot has a mossy right wall.
The climb traverses across this wall low down and then follows
the wall to a junction with Slip Knot, breaking back left to an
overhung corner to finish. Start at the foot of Slip Knot.
1 40 feet. Climb easily up left to a grass ledge below a shallow
   square-cut chimney at the left side of the wall.
2 100 feet (4b). Ascend the chimney for about 15 feet before
   breaking out onto the mossy wall on the right. Traverse across
   to good holds and climb more or less directly up the wall to a
   resting place on the rib (Slip Knot comes in just above). Follow
   a line of large footholds into the the steep groove on the left,
   and after an awkward start, climb it on good holds to a large
   ledge. Continue up the wall to the top.

Shivering Timber   115 feet   Very severe
A 50 foot V-groove with a holly, to the left of Moss Wall, gives
the line of the climb. Quite interesting but short.
1 40 feet. Climb a short wall to gain a scoop. Exit on the left
   and scramble to a stance below the groove.
2 50 feet (4c). Climb the wall left of the groove, until it is possible
   to move right and cross the groove to reach a resting place on
   the right rib. Move back into the bed of the groove and
   climb up to a stance.
3 25 feet. Finish up the short wall above.

Garden Path   150 feet   Very difficult
Roughly follows a slanting rake up the broken-looking buttress with a conspicuous triangular niche in the middle of its steepest section. In its upper half, poor rock abounds and belays are poor. Start at a cairn about 15 feet above the sycamore.
1 60 feet. Climb the wall on good holds past a small ash to a large ledge and gain the obvious rock niche on the left by some awkward moves. Good thread belay in the top left corner.
2 45 feet. Move round the corner on the left to a small ledge; then go right, onto the face above the niche. Continue straight up to a large heather shelf.
3 45 feet. Unpleasant heathery scrambling leads to a large ledge and pinnacle belay. Either escape to the right and finish up the last pitch of Why Not or traverse left to Easy Rake.

Question Not   145 feet   Very difficult
An indefinite line up the right side of the broken scoop, just left of Garden Path. Start a few feet left of Garden Path.
1 55 feet. Climb the rib to a sentry box at 40 feet, then step left into a short, steep V-groove. Above on the right is an apparently sound projecting block. Pull up on this and belay.
2 90 feet. Follow easy slabs and some steeper rock to the top.

Why Not   150 feet   Very difficult
Perhaps the best of the easier climbs in the Ghyll. Start below the scoop just left of Question Not.
1 70 feet. Climb up to a stance level with the holly in Hollin Groove.
2 25 feet. Step right and go up to a break in the overhang above. Climb this with some difficulty to a large ledge.
3 55 feet. Follow steep grass to a huge, detached pinnacle. The groove on the left of the pinnacle leads to the top. Alternatively, step off the pinnacle and climb the slab (severe).

*Hollin Groove   265 feet   Severe
The conspicuous V-groove some 50 feet up the Ghyll from the sycamore. A natural route as far as the Great Shelf, which unfortunately breaks the continuity, although the ridge above is not without interest. Start at the foot of a short, clean groove.
1 75 feet. Climb up the groove, then a rib on the left to another groove, which leads to a belay on the holly.
2 80 feet. Follow the right-angled groove to the Great Shelf. Walk 40 feet to a belay on the rib ahead.
3 35 feet. Go up the steep rib to a spike belay.
4 75 feet. Continue up the rib to the top.

Granny Knot   130 feet   Severe (hard)
A good face climb, quite exposed in its upper section. The overhang is turned on the right unless the easier finish is taken, in which case the standard is Very difficult. Start 30 feet to the left of Hollin Groove, below and to the right of a large rectangular overhang.
1 70 feet. Climb a steep rib to a stance level with a small mountain ash.
2 60 feet. Traverse 15 feet to the right on large holds, then ascend direct over an awkward bulge and continue up an airy ridge to finish on the Great Shelf. Alternatively, climb direct to the overhang from the stance, when a short traverse left leads to easy ground, just below the Great Shelf.

Granny Knot Direct   120 feet   Very severe
Start a few feet left of Hollin Groove, directly below the holly.
1 35 feet. Go up a steep, easy wall to a ledge.
2 85 feet (4b). Step round the corner on the left into a shattered groove and climb up to a large overhang. Step out onto the rib on the right and continue up the splendid finishing wall and awkward bulge of Granny Knot.

Between Granny Knot and the Upper Crag is the well-trodden Easy Rake, leading to the Great Shelf.

Rope Not   55 feet   Very severe (hard)
Above and left of the Great Shelf, a steep 50 foot slab rises from a grassy shelf. The slab is equipped with a tiny overhang just over half-way, and two very thin converging cracks, which give a route of considerable technical charm. Start by scrambling up easy ground to the grassy shelf, though a subsidiary pitch is available above the top of the first part of Easy Rake.
1 55 feet (5b). Climb the cracks with some difficulty.

Hitcher   145 feet   Very severe
The second part of this climb takes the wall left of Rope Not and gives a pitch of unusual character. Start about 25 feet up the Easy Rake, below a short, red, rightward-facing scoop.
1 65 feet (4a). Move up into the scoop, then climb the wall above to the grass shelf. Belay 15 feet higher at the foot of the mossy corner on the left.
2 80 feet (4c). Make a rising traverse across the slab on the right and climb up the far edge to an overhang. Follow the thin crack slanting right above the overhang, to the arête. Go up this for a few feet before traversing back left into a short chimney. Pull out to the right and finish just above.

An unattractive climb, with some doubtful rock, lies up the corner above the first pitch of Hitcher, finishing left under some large overhangs. The standard is Very severe.

Karma 145 feet Extremely severe (E2)
A good, short climb, with a sustained level of technical interest. Start as for Hitcher.
1 65 feet. The red scoop of Hitcher.
2 80 feet (5b). Traverse very steeply left from the foot of the corner, to reach a rib. Climb this with difficulty, to reach the ledge underneath the overhangs. Step boldly right and climb the right wall of a shallow corner.

Upper Crag

**White Ghyll Wall 220 feet Very severe (mild)
The easiest of the routes on the central mass, the overhangs being turned on the right; some fine situations. Start at the foot of a prominent rib, just to the right of a small cave.
1 80 feet. Follow the rib to a ledge beneath the overhangs, then traverse easily right to a stance at the foot of an undercut scoop.
2 50 feet (4b). Climb the scoop, passing an awkward overhang, then step left onto the steep wall and go directly up for 20 feet, when it is possible to move left into a small recess.
3 90 feet (4b). Climb delicately leftwards up the steep slab to a ledge. Easier rocks lead to the top, with a choice of routes.

Tapestry 190 feet Very severe (hard)
A climb with impressive situations but little technical interest, the overhangs being crossed on large doubtful holds. Start about 20 feet left of White Ghyll Wall, directly below an obvious niche set in the lower band of overhangs.
1 70 feet (5a). Follow vegetated rock until a move right can be made onto a rotten ledge just below the niche; pull into it with difficulty, surmount the block above and make an exit, awkwardly to the right. Traverse rightwards to a stance on White Ghyll Wall.
2 50 feet (5a). Climb the overhang above, moving to the right to good holds on the skyline. Pull over to a good ledge on the slab above. Move up to the right hand of two breaks in the overlap and follow this, steeply for a few feet, until it is possible to step left into the fault line leading to a stance on White Ghyll Wall.
3 70 feet (4b). Finish pleasantly up the arête on the left.

Perhaps Not   205 feet   Very severe (hard)

A long traverse left under the overhangs from White Ghyll Wall to reach a break—the notorious chimney pitch! The climb is exposed and quite serious. Start at the foot of the prominent rib, as for White Ghyll Wall.

1 55 feet. Climb the rib to a stance under the overhangs.

2 50 feet (4b). Climb up to the overhang and traverse left underneath it to the foot of an overhung chimney.

3 30 feet (5a). The chimney is climbed with some difficulty, (faith in what may be above is required when the holds disappear) until a step out to the right can be made below the overhang; then go up to a stance.

4 70 feet (4b). Continue straight up the wall to finish.

Eliminot   210 feet   Extremely severe (E2)

A difficult and interesting route, the climbing being both fierce and technically demanding. The line unfortunately is rather contrived, the lower half constituting a direct start to Perhaps Not and the upper half an indirect finish. Start at the foot of a narrow slab which runs in a single sweep up to the main overhang.

1 75 feet (5b). Climb the slab (as for Gordian Knot) for about 30 feet. Traverse right, under a barrier of overhangs, to a ledge under a niche, set in the overhangs. Pull over the overhang and climb the niche to a resting place. Continue steeply to the stance below the chimney of Perhaps Not.

2 65 feet (5b). Go down to the right, reversing part of the traverse of Perhaps Not, until it is possible to pull up round an awkward bulge (poor rock) onto another long thin slab, sandwiched between overhangs. Climb up through a break in the overhangs above and, after a move or two left, pull over a small overlap and continue to a stance (junction with Perhaps Not).

3 70 feet (4b). Continue up the wall to finish.

**The Gordian Knot   195 feet   Very severe

A natural climb of great character; the second pitch is not won easily at first acquantance. Start at the foot of the narrow slab, as for Eliminot.

1 65 feet (4b). Go straight up the slab, then step left and continue up to a cave stance.

2 50 feet (4c). Make an easy traverse to the right for 15 feet to a good ledge below a mossy corner. Climb the corner, until it is possible to gain a tiny ledge on the right wall. Pull up on good holds and move back left into a recess. Continue up strenuously to a good stance.

3 80 feet (4b). Finish up the wall above.

*White Ghyll Eliminate   190 feet   Extremely severe (E2)
The main pitch, though short, is very steep, strenuous and exhilarating and the climb as a whole gives a very direct way up the
crag. Start as for Gordian Knot.
1 65 feet (4b). Climb the slab as for Gordian Knot.
2 50 feet (5c). Pull up steeply into the crack above and follow
   it with difficulty to a stance on the Haste Not traverse.
3 75 feet (5a). Step left and climb the awkward crack, splitting
   the overhang. Continue up the pleasant slabs above to finish.

*Haste Not Direct   155 feet   Extremely severe (E2)
Another good, steep, direct route through the overhangs, the
bulging crack being particularly sensational. Start at the foot of
a rather gloomy corner left of Gordian Knot.
1 70 feet (4c). Climb directly to the roof which closes the corner
   and exit right onto the rib. Move right again to belay as for
   Gordian Knot.
2 85 feet (5c). Move up through the overhangs to a slim groove
   and, after a few feet, pull out left to a resting place. Continue
   up steeply, to reach the traverse of Haste Not. Climb the
   bulging crack, which proves both awkward and very strenuous.

**Haste Not   190 feet   Very severe
A very fine climb up the overhung walls on the left of Gordian
Knot. Interest is well maintained and the level of exposure is
high. Start about 20 feet left of Gordian Knot at the foot of a
short overhung slab.
1 70 feet (4b). Follow the slab easily to an inverted V overhang
   and gain the big slab on the front by an awkward traverse
   across the wall on the left. Once on the front, go up a shallow
   groove, over an awkward bulge to a ledge and belays.
2 50 feet (4c). Traverse easily rightwards until it is possible to
   climb a steep wall, which gives access to a gangway running
   right under the big overhang. Traverse the gangway and make
   a difficult move across a bottomless groove. Continue round a
   rib and belay as for White Ghyll Eliminate.
3 70 feet (4b). Make an awkward move above the stance and
   continue between two overhanging blocks to the top.

To the left of Haste Not, the overhangs become particularly
impressive and they are breached by a number of sensational
climbs, all of which start from a ledge and block belay 45 feet
up White Ghyll Chimney, the obvious fault which marks the
termination of the central part of the crag.

Horror   130 feet   Extremely severe (E3)
An intimidating and sustained piece of climbing.
1 70 feet (6a). Climb easy rocks to the right to the bottom of a
  very steep corner (Paladin). Continue rightwards to a position
  above the traverse of Haste Not. Swing out right and pull up
  through the overhangs to a peg runner, on the left. Go up
  through more overhanging rock to easy ground.
2 60 feet. Finish easily.

*Paladin   110 feet   Extremely severe (E3)
The impressive overhanging corner gives a superb route; the
technical difficulty is nowhere excessive but the climbing is
sustained and strenuous.
1 80 feet (5c). Move up rightwards to the foot of the corner; step
  left and climb a slab and then a bulging wall until it is possible
  to move into the corner below a roof. Move right round the
  roof and pull up steeply into a niche. Make a few awkward
  moves left to a subsidiary groove and climb this to a stance.
2 30 feet. Follow easy ground to the top.

Warrior   110 feet   Extremely severe (E4)
A contrived line through the overhangs left of Paladin, giving
sustained and interesting climbing.
1 110 feet (6a). Climb Paladin for a few feet, then step left and
  move onto a short slab with difficulty; cross the slab and pull
  out leftwards. Continue to the traverse of Chimney Variant.
  Move left and climb through bulges to a groove. Ascend the
  wall on the right and go slightly left to more overhangs. Move
  right to finish at the top of Paladin.

The Rampant Finish   (6a)
Traverse back left from the belay, peg runner, and pull up to
reach holds above the roof. Move left, peg runner, and climb
a rib and cracks to the top.

*Chimney Variant   115 feet   Extremely severe (E1)
Superb climbing with exciting situations.
1 90 feet (5b). Climb up to the overhang in White Ghyll chimney;
  pull over it and move right to the obvious undercut gangway,
  which leads to the foot of a fine little groove. Follow this
  groove with difficulty, until it is possible to step out to the
  rib on the right; move up to a small stance a little higher.
2 25 feet. Finish up the easier groove above.

*White Ghyll Chimney   185 feet   Severe
A classic route of considerable character up the pronounced cleft between the central overhangs and the Slabs. Start at the foot of the cleft.
1 65 feet. Climb easily up the bed of a groove to a terrace. Walk up to a thread belay in the Sentry Box, above which the chimney narrows to a crack.
2 80 feet. Ascend the cave for 10 feet and make a very awkward movement to a sloping hold on the left. Balance over to reach small handholds and continue more easily up a steep groove, trending leftwards, to a grass ledge. 20 feet further up this is a good belay.
2a A more difficult, but often drier, alternative is to avoid the chimney entirely by climbing the wall on its left. From the belay in the Sentry Box step down a few feet and traverse left across the wall for 15 feet. A direct ascent on smaller holds then leads to the same diagonal groove.
3 40 feet. Return 10 feet from the belay and ascend the wall above for 15 feet. A delicate traverse leads back into the chimney, which is followed to the top.

Dead Loss Angeles   120 feet   Extremely severe (E3)†
A serious route up the featureless wall, left of White Ghyll Chimney. The line goes between two moss streaks in the upper half of the crag. Start about 15 feet left of the chimney.
1 120 feet (5b). Climb easily to a break and follow a vague groove to a spike. Climb the bulge above to a ledge on White Ghyll Traverse. Gain another ledge above and climb up to ledges and the top.

A route known as **Runner Wall** goes up the slab immediately left of Dead Loss Angeles. The climbing is characterless, the interest fair, the rock rather friable and the standard Very severe.

**The Slabs, Route 1   225 feet   Severe
Both the Slab routes offer pleasant climbing on steep, sound rock, well supplied with holds. Route 1 is, perhaps, the harder. Start at the lowest part of the buttress.
1 40 feet. Follow bubbly rocks to a ledge with a belay at its left end.
2 50 feet. Traverse upwards across the wall on the left to a small ledge. Climb the steep groove above, until a move can be made out to the right to a splendid spike belay.
3 55 feet. Make an awkward start up the wall, 10 feet left of the belay, and continue on better holds to the middle one of three grooves. Follow this, and another groove slightly right, to the terrace which runs out from White Ghyll Chimney.
4 80 feet. Follow the steep rib slightly right of the belay to the top.

*The Slabs, Route 2   145 feet   Severe
Start at the left end of the buttress, below its bounding ridge.
1 35 feet. Climb a steep crack, just to the right, to a stance on
   Route 1.
2 30 feet. Traverse horizontally left across the wall, until a good
   hold facilitates a pull onto the slab above. Continue diagonally
   right to the good spike belay on Route 1.
3 45 feet. Reverse Pitch 2 for 20 feet and climb the wall above by
   means of a crack running diagonally left; the ridge further left
   leads to a stance.
4 35 feet. Follow the ridge on the right of the grassy scoop.
   Scrambling leads to the top.

Variation start   65 feet
Rather harder than the original route. Start at the foot of an
open chimney on the immediate left of the Slabs proper.
1a 65 feet. Climb the chimney until it is possible to step out
    onto the slab on the left. Traverse right along ledges and
    across a delicate slab to a junction with the parent climb.
    Continue up this to the spike belay.

White Ghyll Traverse   715 feet   Very severe
An attractive expedition, offering a fair taste of some of the best
climbing on the crag. The easiest practicable line is followed from
Hollin Groove to the far edge of the Slabs. Start at the foot of
Hollin Groove.
1 & 2 155 feet (4a). The first two pitches of Hollin Groove to the
       Great Shelf.
3   50 feet. Scramble easily up to a block belay above the
       first steep section of Easy Rake.
4   70 feet. Take the easiest line leftwards to the block belay
       at the foot of Pitch 2, White Ghyll Wall.
5   110 feet (4b). Follow White Ghyll Wall to the ledge below
       the final easy section.
6   40 feet (4a). Climb down diagonally left to the top of the
       crux pitch of Gordian Knot.
7   50 feet (4c). Descend the corner (crux) and move left to
       the cave stance.
8   45 feet (4b). Traverse left from the cave across the top of
       an undercut groove and so to a slab, which is climbed to
       its top left hand corner.
9   25 feet. Make an easy traverse to a block belay just right
       of the chimney.
10   90 feet (4c). Continue the traverse with difficulty, first
       ascending to a shattered ledge, then descending delicately

to the arête, whence good holds lead diagonally left to
the spike belay on Slabs Route 1.

11   45 feet (4a). Traverse left to belay on Slabs Route 2.
12   35 feet (4a). Follow the rib on the right of the grassy
      scoop. Scrambling leads to the top.

Variation Girdle Traverse   420 feet   Extremely severe (E1)
An alternative girdle of the Upper Crag. An enjoyable outing
with some excellent situations. On pitch 2, the descent of a short
section of Eliminot demands a bold approach from the last man.
Start as for Hitcher.

1 90 feet (4a). Climb Pitch 1 of Hitcher and traverse easily left
   to belay below Pitch 2 of White Ghyll Wall.
2 100 feet (5a). Pull over the first overhang, as for White Ghyll
   Wall, and then traverse the long sandwiched slab on the left.
   Where the overhangs above and below meet, it is necessary
   to descend the bottom one (reversing part of Eliminot) to
   gain the traverse of Perhaps Not. Follow this to the stance
   below the chimney.
3 50 feet (4c). Step down and traverse awkwardly across to
   Gordian Knot. Ascend the mossy corner and go up to belay at
   the end of the Haste Not traverse.
4 60 feet (4c). Reverse the traverse of Haste Not and continue
   into White Ghyll Chimney.
5 120 feet (4a). Finish up White Ghyll Chimney.

Swine Knott

This is the steep little outcrop on the left of the entrance to
White Ghyll. A few climbs have been made but they do not
merit description.

PAVEY ARK (286080)

From the Stickle Barn in Great Langdale, Pavey Ark is approached by ascending Mill Ghyll. There is a track on each side of the ghyll, but the one on the true right side is more commonly used. On reaching Stickle Tarn, the crag appears in full view. From here the drier and shorter route is on the left of the tarn, and afterwards, indefinite tracks lead up the scree to the foot of the crag.

The crag in general faces south and enjoys rather more sun and more varied vegetation than most of the Lakeland crags. It is the largest cliff in Langdale, a factor which, together with its fine situation above Stickle Tarn, compensates for the occasional shortcomings of the rock itself (though these are more apparent than real). It is split by gullies into several distinct buttresses. Those to the left of Great Gully, the second deeply-cut gully from the left, are neither steep nor sound, but broken and unsuitable for good climbing. Stony Buttress comes next between Great Gully and a shallow, dirt-filled groove, which marks the line of ascent to the Crescent (the signs of a rock fall are still visible hereabouts). Next comes a sweep of smooth slabs, bordered above and down to the right by a series of grassy ledges, which form a rake (Jack's Rake) leading from high up on the western end of the crags down to the scree at the eastern extremity. Above Jack's Rake, the crag, bounded on its right by the well-defined Rake End Chimney and on the left by the upper reaches of Great Gully, is covered with much vegetation. Despite this there are many rock walls and buttresses, which rise steeply from the surrounding heather and provide remarkably clean and attractive climbing. Cook's Tour and Golden Slipper are good examples.

Beyond Rake End Chimney, the East Buttress forms a large area of steep rock. The structure is one of smooth, mossy slabs and bulges, and except for the pillar on the immediate right of the chimney, does not dry quickly. The right-hand wing of the East Buttress bends round and becomes the East Wall (the pride of Pavey Ark), in effect a gully wall, but with the other side so low as to be almost non-existent. The crag here is impressively steep and smooth with very few horizontal breaks (Hobson's Choice being the only real one). Climbs are bigger and more serious on this side of the crag.

Many climbs lead only to Jack's Rake, which serves as an easy means of descent. From the summit a descent can be made round either extremity, or, more easily, via the easier upper section of Great Gully to Jack's Rake and then down the latter. Rake End Chimney provides a pleasant means of descent after climbing on the eastern end of the crag, though care is needed to avoid dislodging scree on to ascending parties. The climbs, which may be divided into three sections, viz, those below Jack's Rake, those above, and those on the East Wall, are described from left to right.

Climbs below Jack's Rake

Little Gully   350 feet   Moderate
This is the most westerly gully. Start by scrambling up the gully to the fork at about 200 feet. The difficulties, such as they are, commence 50 feet up the right hand branch.
1 100 feet. Climb the gully; excursions on to each wall in turn being necessary at various points.

*Great Gully   330 feet   Difficult
This is the right and longer one of the two deeply-marked gullies towards the western end of the crag. One of the few good gully climbs in the district.
1 150 feet. Follow easy rocks for 40 feet and then scramble to a cave beneath a large chockstone.
2 35 feet. Climb the wall on the right.
3 60 feet. Scramble up to a cave and climb through or over it.
4 65 feet. Climb the pleasant slab.
5 20 feet. Take either a very difficult scoop on the left, an easy through route, or an easy grass exit on the right. These all lead to Jack's Rake, which can be followed up or down, or the grassy gully on the right can be taken to the summit.

Stony Buttress   370 feet   Severe
The climb lies on the buttress to the right of Great Gully. A disappointing climb, serious and with some loose rock. Start by scrambling up heather for 60 feet to a ledge on the edge of Great Gully.
1 40 feet. Climb diagonally to the right.
2 50 feet. Continue upwards to the right until, after rounding a corner and taking a step up, a ledge is reached with a belay on the right.
3 40 feet. Climb the obvious steep groove (poor rock) and break out on to steep grass ledges on the left.

4 70 feet. Step right and then work back leftwards through the bilberries.
5 100 feet. Follow pastures to a corner.
6 70 feet. Climb onto the ledge on the right. Go up the steep little ridge to another large ledge and continue up another ridge to join Jack's Rake.

The Hobbit 190 feet Extremely severe (E2)
A steep and serious climb with both poor rock and protection, which takes an impressive line around the overhangs on the front of Stony Buttress. Start about 50 feet up the gully to the left of Crescent Climb, on the left bounding rib of the obvious wet black groove.
1 120 feet (5b). Move onto the rib just above some bushes, and climb this until level with the lower overhang. Move right, and climb up for 15 feet past a wedged flake. Gain the ledge on the left with difficulty; then traverse horizontally left for 10 feet until a steep crack is reached. Climb the crack to a ledge with a juniper. Move right, and climb the groove, bearing left to spike belays.
2 70 feet. Climb the vegetated rocks to finish.

Sinistral 120 feet Extremely severe (E1)
A less worthy companion to The Hobbit. Start as for The Hobbit.
1 120 feet (5a). Move up the rib, as for The Hobbit, to the obvious horizontal break under the first overhang. Follow this break left for 30 feet, to the foot of a short overhanging corner. Climb this and move left to a tiny ledge. Climb cracks to an overhang and traverse left to a ledge on Stony Buttress.

The Ragman's Trumpet 290 feet Extremely severe (E2)
A serious route up the impressive crack in the right wall of Stony Buttress. The wall is steep and the climbing strenuous and sustained. Start about 50 feet up the gully right of Stony Buttress, just below a little cave pitch.
1 100 feet (5b). Go up and across the wall on the left to gain the crack, just above the black groove. Follow the crack, first directly upwards, and then to the right as it slants across the wall, to gain the ledge at the top. The pull-out is best made on the right.
2 190 feet. Climb the much easier ground above, or finish up Sally Free and Easy.

Variation
A direct start is available up the black groove directly below the crack, but this is usually wet.

Sally Free and Easy 170 feet Extremely severe (E2)
This is really Crescent Gully direct, but it can be conveniently linked with The Ragman's Trumpet, and is described that way. A serious climb with loose rock and poor protection. Start from the top of pitch 1 of The Ragman's Trumpet.

1 35 feet (5a). Make an awkward rising traverse to the right into the big corner. Peg belays.
2 135 feet (5c). Follow the corner on poor rock to a niche below the final overhanging crack. Climb this for a few feet and exit left with difficulty onto a ledge. Ascend easily to a spike belay on Jack's Rake.

Crescent Climb 330 feet Moderate
The broken arête to the right of Crescent Gully, leads to an exposed traverse across the top of Crescent Slabs. The lower section is quite loose and requires care. Start at the foot of the gully.

1 180 feet. Follow the arête to a ledge with a flake above, at the left end of the Crescent. Stances and doubtful belays *en route*.
2 50 feet. Make a pleasant traverse to the right on large holds under the overhang.
3 100 feet. Go up grassy slabs to join Jack's Rake.

Crescent Wall 200 feet Severe
A rather indefinite route on the steep mossy slabs to the right of the first section of Crescent Climb. Disappointing, but finishes well. Start about 50 feet to the right of Crescent Climb, below easy rocks.

1 35 feet. Go diagonally left to a ledge.
2 100 feet. Climb the steep rocks above, moving left or right, as difficulty indicates, until a grassy traverse leads across to a large sloping ledge on the right.
3 65 feet. Climb the corner; then continue straight up clean slabs to the Crescent.

*Crescent Slabs 200 feet Severe
Follows a line roughly parallel to Crescent Wall up the clean open slabs on the right of the moss. A very good climb of its type on excellent rock. Start at an obvious weakness at the right end of the slabs.

1 40 feet. Follow a rising gangway to the left. This is usually wet.
2 40 feet. Traverse obliquely right into a shallow groove. Ascend this for a few feet before working left over easier slabs to a spike belay.
Alternatively, and more easily, traverse horizontally left and climb a slab.

3 60 feet. Go up steep slabs to a ledge and step right below a block. Make a difficult move up from the block into a small scoop, then, after a few feet, move left to a small ledge.
Alternatively, make a rising traverse left and then move back right to the small ledge; this is not easy either.

4 60 feet. Climb pleasant slabs to join the Crescent Climb.

Crescent Direct 90 feet Very severe
The shallow groove up the right side of the buttress above the Crescent. Start from the good flake at the right end of the traverse of Crescent Climb. This is easily reached from Jack's Rake, or by first climbing Wailing Wall or Crescent Slabs.

1 60 feet (4b). Make some awkward moves up into the groove and climb it for about 40 feet, when it is possible to traverse horizontally left onto a grass ledge on the front of the buttress.

2 30 feet (4b). Climb the steep slabs starting from the left.

Wailing Wall 170 feet Very severe (mild)
Beyond Crescent Slabs the main, or central, buttress assumes the steepness of a wall, characterised by an obvious stratum of rock, the Barrier, at its foot. An obvious corner running up the left side of this steeper section marks the line. On the whole the climb is undistinguished and, though interesting in parts, is grassy and often wet. Start a few feet to the right of Crescent Slabs below an undercut groove.

1 25 feet (4c). Climb the Barrier (very low here) and then the awkward groove to a small stance.

2 40 feet (4a). Traverse right into a groove and continue to a gangway running up to the left. Follow this to its left end, when a stride is made to a ledge with a large flake belay.

3 60 feet (4b). Go up the corner on the right, past a smooth section, to a small stance.

4 45 feet (4b). Start just to the right of the corner, where two awkward steps bring better holds within reach. Continue up short steep walls to a ledge at about 30 feet and then traverse left into a corner. Jack's Rake can be reached by about 100 feet of scrambling.

Alph 275 feet Very severe
Right of Wailing Wall, the cliff steepens a little and becomes less grassy. The route avoids the main steepness by a long upward traverse to the right; then it breaks back to easier and grassier ground. A wandering sort of climb, but pleasant and open and, except for the start, without gymnastics. Start a few feet to the left of Wailing Wall.

1 35 feet (4b). Ascend the Barrier and then the overhang, where

it is broken by a shallow depression (10 feet right of Wailing Wall). Traverse right to the stance at the top of Pitch 1, Wailing Wall.

2 80 feet (4b). Make a rising traverse to the right on rather sloping holds, to reach a small ledge with a holly.

3 65 feet (4c). Step down to the left and make an awkward move out onto the left wall. Traverse delicately left for a few feet to a shallow groove, which is ascended to a small juniper ledge. Traverse left again to a ledge, then go up to another ledge. Climb the rib at the left end of the ledge for about 10 feet, when a horizontal traverse can be made back to the right to a good ledge.

4 95 feet (4a). Traverse right for a few feet, then climb towards Jack's Rake via short walls and grooves, alternating with grass ledges.

Variation   Direct Start   35 feet   Very severe (hard)
A good pitch, which is surprisingly difficult. Start below a smooth looking groove right of the start of Wailing Wall. It is the last obvious break through the Barrier on this side of the crag.
1a 35 feet (5b). Climb the groove.

Variation
2a 105 feet (4c). Steeper and more direct than the original pitch. Go up left for a few feet, as for Wailing Wall, then climb directly up, via a 'pocket' wall, to the right end of a sloping ledge. Traverse right to reach a shallow crack line, and climb it to a small ledge. Step right to a junction with Alph, then go up left to a large ledge. Climb up again at the left end and go back to the right to the top of Pitch 3 of Alph.

Arcturus   270 feet   Very severe (hard)
A fine open climb with excellent situations. The route takes the steep two-tier wall to the left of the big slabby break of Deception. Start near the foot of Deception.

1 115 feet (5a). Climb the Barrier to the foot of the groove of Deception. Ascend the wall on the left, which guards access to the slab, and after about 12 feet step left to a large foothold. Move delicately up the slab, bearing left past a peg, to a tiny ledge, invisible from below. Avoid the smooth section immediately above by working left into a thin crack, which leads to a shallow niche and a stance on Alph, just above.

2 65 feet (5a). Pull over the small overlap on the right and climb a shallow groove to a small ledge. Step back into the line of the

groove and climb the thin crack to a narrow ledge, with a large ledge a little higher.

3 90 feet (5a). Follow a narrow ledge along to the right beneath the overlap; continue the traverse across a delicate little slab (exposed) to a ledge. Step down and go to the right end of the large ledge below, where a rib leads to easier ground and a belay. Scramble up to Jack's Rake.

Big Brother   240 feet   Extremely severe (E3)

A big serious pitch up the wall right of Arcturus. Start as for Arcturus.

1 100 feet (5a). Follow Arcturus to a small ledge above the peg and move up rightwards to a good ledge below the obvious shallow groove. Climb this to the ledge under the overhang and traverse right a few feet to belay. (Cruel Sister Pitch 1.)

2 90 feet (5c). Traverse left a few feet, pull over the overhang at a thin crack and follow this to where it fades. Move left at a thin horizontal crack, then go rightwards to good holds at the base of a short corner. Climb this and continue in the same line to join the Arcturus traverse.

3 50 feet (5a). Finish up either Arcturus or Cruel Sister.

***Cruel Sister   230 feet   Extremely severe (E3)

A technical and absorbing climb, which follows the superb undercut rib forming the right-hand side of the upper wall. Protection is adequate and the difficulties are at the lower limit of the grade. Start as for Arcturus.

1 100 feet (5a). Follow Arcturus to a small ledge above the peg and move up rightwards to a good ledge below the obvious shallow groove. Climb this to the ledge under the overhang and traverse right a few feet to belay.

2 80 feet (5c). Pull over the overhang and move up to reach a peg. Step up, traverse right to a block on the edge, and then go up to a good foothold. Climb the wall trending slightly left to a small overlap. Surmount this and gain a steep crack-line which leads to the good ledge at the end of the Arcturus traverse. A magnificent pitch.

3 50 feet (5a). Move left, and crossing Arcturus, pull over the overlap on widely spaced holds. Step left and climb the obvious corner to grass ledges. Move right and back left onto the second ledge for belays.

Deception 180 feet Severe

The route follows the grassy corner on the right of the central wall. Vegetated and often wet or greasy but with some interesting moves. Start below the Barrier, a little right of the corner.

1 20 feet. Climb the Barrier to the ledge below the overhang; then walk left along the ledge to the foot of the groove.
2 115 feet. Climb the groove to a good spike and step right to grassy rocks, which are ascended to a ledge in the corner. Work diagonally right over grass ledges, then go straight up to a large ledge at the foot of a slab.
3 45 feet. Climb the slab at its left corner and make a delicate traverse right to a good ledge, with a good thread belay in the niche above on the left. Jack's Rake is a few feet higher on the right.

Variation start 120 feet Severe

A drier alternative to the usual start. Start about 12 yards right of the normal start, where a block leans against the face.

1 120 feet. Follow an obvious curving line up to the belay below the last pitch.

The Rainmaker 105 feet Extremely severe (E1)

A fine steep pitch with splendid holds, except for the start, which is hard. The open corner in the steep wall above and left of Deception. Start from the top of Pitch 2 of Deception.

1 105 feet (5b). Go up to the left and gain a tiny undercut glacis at the foot of the corner. Follow a small subsidiary corner on the left to a small ledge and step across to a small pinnacle on the right. Continue, more easily now, to easy ground at the top of Arcturus.

Obscured by Clouds 100 feet Extremely severe (E3)†

A short serious pitch taking the shallow groove and crack in the wall right of Rainmaker. Start at the top of Pitch 2 of Deception.

1 100 feet (5c). Climb the obvious steep, shallow groove and pull over the bulge with difficulty. Follow the crack above to a grass terrace. Step immediately left, around the rib, at a loose block, and continue up the short corner and wall above to the top.

Climbs above Jack's Rake

Little Corner   120 feet   Very severe (hard)
This climb and the following one are high up at the western end
of the crag, just left of the big obvious rock-fall scar on the left
of the crescent. A fine corner, which will be enjoyable if it ever
becomes clean. Start at the foot of a slab below the corner.
1 120 feet (5a). Go up the slab to the right one of twin grooves
   forming the corner. Climb this for about 25 feet, then transfer
   to the left one, which is followed until a good flake-crack on
   the left wall leads to a pinnacle, and an opportunity to swing
   out of the corner on to the left-hand rib. Climb up a further
   20 feet to finish.

Roundabout   170 feet   Severe
A prominent, thin leftward-facing crack, about 60 feet up, marks
the line. A somewhat indirect route. It almost becomes submerged
in heather towards the middle, but later, a delightful little airy
rib gives it definition. Start at a cairn about 50 yards left of
Gwynne's Chimney.
1 40 feet. Go up to a slabby scoop and follow this to a large
   juniper below the thin crack.
2 45 feet. Move up to the foot of the crack and traverse across
   the foot of the buttress on the right on a grassy gangway.
   Climb a shallow square-cut chimney round the corner to a
   stance on the left.
3 85 feet. Step off from the embedded flake and climb up the
   left edge of the clean rib. Finish up a series of short steep walls.

Roundabout Direct   200 feet   Very severe
The steep corner crack directly above the slabby scoop of Roundabout. Start from the top of the first pitch of Roundabout.
1 120 feet (4c). Climb the corner until, at about 40 feet, it is
   possible to step left onto easier angled slabs. Go up these to a
   niche beneath the overhangs and pull round to the right.
   Move up to a ledge and continue up a couple of short walls
   on the left to a belay.
2 80 feet. Follow ledges and walls to the top.

*Golden Slipper   200 feet   Very severe (hard)

A slim elegant pillar, left of the obvious dark corner, provides an airy and enjoyable climb of considerable charm on perfect rock. Start about 20 yards left of Gwynne's Chimney at a gangway slanting right to a line of small overhangs at 20 feet.

1 60 feet (4b). Follow the gangway, easily, to the overhang and step right onto a ledge. Climb directly up the steep wall above to another ledge and belay at the foot of the slab.

2 80 feet (4c). Climb directly up the slab on superbly rough rock until the slab becomes a wall. Traverse across to the rib on the right and ascend this to a large ledge.

3 60 feet (4a). Go up the rib to the slab on the left and follow it to the top.

A poor climb has been made following a line left of Golden Slipper.

Poker Face   270 feet   Extremely severe (E1)

A slim groove in the edge separating Golden Slipper from Troll's Corner. It is steep and interesting. Start 5 yards left of Gwynne's Chimney.

1 120 feet (4b). Go up easily to a ledge on the left. Climb the slabby corner, past a holly, to another ledge with a block. Continue straight up from the block and, after about 15 feet, traverse left to the belay of Golden Slipper.

2 90 feet (5b). Go up slabby rock to the right into a thin groove on the edge of the buttress. Climb the groove (difficult and sustained) until the crack steepens considerably about 10 feet below the top, where it is possible to make a difficult move onto Golden Slipper. Follow this to the large ledge.

3 60 feet (4a). Climb the rib on the left (as for Golden Slipper).

Troll's Corner   215 feet   Very severe (hard)

The obvious dark corner, rising from a large grassy bay on the left of Gwynne's Chimney. The corner itself overhangs, is often damp, and the climbing is very strenuous. Start at the foot of Gwynne's Chimney.

1 115 feet (4c). Move up to the big bluebell ledge on the left and continue up the slabs, with one or two awkward moves. Go directly up the steep wall for 15 feet, until it is possible to make an awkward move onto an obvious traverse line. Follow this to a ledge in the corner.

2 50 feet (5a). Climb directly up the impending corner and, where the left wall drops back at 25 feet, make an awkward pull onto a tiny slab. Move up easily to a stance.

3 50 feet (4b). Climb the steep wall and finish up a slab.

Stalag 220 feet Very severe
An escape route from Troll's Corner, interesting but without much direction. Start as for Troll's Corner.
1 115 feet (4c). As for Troll's Corner.
2 50 feet (4b). Traverse the sharp-edged flake across the steep right wall to reach a comfortable niche. Continue along the traverse to a small ledge, when it is possible to go up a short wall to a stance.
3 55 feet (4b). Climb the steep little slab on the left to a small exposed ledge; continue over a small ledge to a pile of blocks. Swing round the rib on the left and follow it to the top.

Gwynne's Chimney 80 feet Difficult
A pleasant little chimney. Start from Jack's Rake a few feet to the right of the end of The Crescent.
1 80 feet. Climb the chimney, which may be quitted after about 55 feet for the right rib, or for grassier ground further right. If desired, the climb may be extended by following the well scratched route to the summit or by traversing right to finish up the last two pitches of Cook's Tour.

Aardvark 180 feet Extremely severe (E1)
The steep arête to the right of Gwynne's Chimney. Start 30 feet down to the right of Gwynne's Chimney on a small quartz glacis.
1 110 feet (5c). Climb straight up to a peg below a small overhang. Move left and up, with difficulty, to reach a sloping ledge. Make an awkward move up rightwards across a wall to a small spike on the arête. Follow the arête to a ledge and spike belay.
2 70 feet. Climb a short wall on the right to meet Cook's Tour. Move right again and climb the obvious crack to slabs and the top.

Rectangular Slab 200 feet Very severe
The big slab set at right angles to the cliff. An interesting climb with sizable stances and a fine slab pitch. Start from Jack's Rake, rather less than halfway down from Gwynne's Chimney to Rake End Chimney, at a shallow rightward facing corner.
1 50 feet (4c). Climb the left-hand rib to an obvious projecting block at the foot of two grooves. Ascend the left-hand one to the big terrace, moving out onto the steep left wall for the last few feet.
Walk round to the right to belay below the Rectangular Slab.
2 115 feet (4b). Climb the corner past a holly to reach a fine traverse line, which is followed to the left edge of the slab. Ascend the slab using a thin crack to a steep finish.
3 35 feet (5a). Go up an easy slab to a steep little crack. Climb this with difficulty to a good belay.

Rectangular Rib 130 feet Very severe (hard)
Pleasant climbing up the left edge of Rectangular Slab. It can be reached by a long and slightly descending traverse from the top of The Rib Pitch. Start below the left edge of the slab.
1 80 feet (5a). Make some thin moves up to the slab. Follow the left edge of the slab to a ledge.
2 50 feet (4c). Follow short walls and slabs to the top.

Cook's Tour 295 feet Very difficult
The pitches are short and the belays good, the route being suitable for an inexperienced party. Start at a short easy chimney-crack, leftward facing and roughly half-way between Gwynne's Chimney and Rake End Chimney. The chimney-crack is the first obviously easy break in the rocks to the right of Gwynne's Chimney.
1 55 feet. Climb the open groove to a platform and continue up the steep slab, moving round to the right onto the top of a pinnacle.
2 45 feet. Follow easy climbing and steep bracken to a flake-belay at the foot of an imposing slab.
3 75 feet. Move up to a large grass ledge, 25 feet away and walk along it for 50 feet to a flake-belay below an open grassy gully.
4 35 feet. Climb the gully and move right to a grass ledge. Traverse to the right, past a flake and continue up to a pleasant grassy corner.
5 85 feet. Ascend the crack to the top of the flake and continue up the steep slab to a good ledge. Finish up the wall above, first slightly right, then straight up.

Bracken Route 380 feet Severe
Well named! It offers only a little rock and the best of that belongs to Cook's Tour. Start as for that route.
1 100 feet. The first two pitches of Cook's Tour.
2 90 feet. Climb to the right of the big slab for 20 feet, then go up to a ledge on the right. Traverse the ledge to its right hand end, when a 15-foot descent leads to a ledge.
3 30 feet. Traverse the heather to below a corner.
4 60 feet. Climb the corner for 30 feet and step right onto the arête. Go up this to a good stance by some jammed quartz blocks.
5 30 feet. Make a rising traverse right to a large pinnacle.
6 70 feet. Climb the steep face behind the belay as direct as possible. Finish up the easier ground above.

Chequer Buttress 210 feet Very severe (hard)
The buttress flanking Rake End Chimney; it has some loose rock but also a sound crux in a good position. Start at the foot of Rake End Chimney.
1 50 feet. Go up and round to the left to a steep herbaceous groove, which is ascended to a small stance.
2 70 feet (5a). Traverse across the bulging wall; then climb a steep, delicate little slab on the right edge overlooking the chimney and swing back left into a shallow corner. Continue directly up to a tiny ledge, then another with a tree on the left. Belay behind the tree in a cave.
3 85 feet (4c). Climb the edge of the steep slab on the right to grassy scrambling, which leads to a narrow overhanging crack. Follow this until a pull out can be made to the right, step back left and climb up to the top.

Variation finish 130 feet Very severe
An open and attractive way of finishing the climb.
3a 130 feet (4b). Make a rising traverse out to the rib on the right, step round the corner and join The Rib Pitch just above its crux; follow it to the top .

The Rib 220 feet Extremely severe (E1)
Some interesting climbing and good situations, although rather close to Rake End Chimney in places. Start at the foot of Rake End Chimney.
1 50 feet (5c). Traverse horizontally left from the foot of the steep part of the chimney to just below a small niche. Step up and left, and climb up with difficulty, avoiding leftward possibilities, to a hollow flake and a small stance above on the left.
2 170 feet (5a). Move back right (as for Chequer Buttress) and go up to the arête. Follow the groove, overlooking the chimney, to a difficult pull-out onto a slab. Climb this to the superb rib (The Rib Pitch) and finish up this. It is possible to split the pitch at a block about 20 feet below the top.

**Rake End Chimney 235 feet Difficult
An excellent chimney climb. Start at the foot of Jake's Rake.
1 35 feet. Go up easy steps to the chimney proper.
2 65 feet. Climb the chimney past two ledges and over a chockstone.
3 70 feet. Walk up the gully.
4 65 feet. Climb up to and through the window and then go up the right wall to a small cave. Pass this on the left to finish easily.

Directly in front is a short wall of about 45 feet containing two cracks. The right-hand one provides an interesting pitch of about Severe standard.

Death Star 220 feet Extremely severe (E3)
The right hand rib of Rake End Chimney gives a very serious pitch. Start at the foot of the rib.
1 120 feet (5c). Follow the right-hand side of the black moss streak and move right to a thin crack. Climb this to a ledge; pull over the bulge very close to Rake End Wall and continue up the rib to a stance in the chimney.
2 100 feet (5a). Climb the left wall of Rake End Chimney to a slab which leads to near the top of The Rib Pitch. Finish up this.

**Rake End Wall 210 feet Very severe
Enjoyable and sustained climbing on excellent rock, marred only by its junction with Rake End Chimney. Start 5 yards right of the the chimney.
1 70 feet (4b). Climb a rib past a wedged flake and go up an ill-defined crack until its steepening necessitates a move round the corner to the right. Follow a diagonal crack to the huge block below an overhanging corner, with a stance on the right.
2 35 feet (4c). Climb the imposing crack in the corner to a ledge, with a belay 10 feet higher.
3 65 feet (4b). Step round to the left from the lower end of the ledge, onto a fine slab. Ascend directly to the right of a slight overhang and make an awkward move to the arête on the left, which leads to the large terrace below the final pitch of Rake End Chimney.
4 40 feet (4a). Climb the left edge of the right-bounding wall of the chimney, with a detour to the right to avoid the steepest section.

By-Pass Route 175 feet Very severe (hard)
A series of variations on Rake End Wall. Start from a narrow ledge below the groove coming down in the line of the over-hanging crack of Rake End Wall.
1 70 feet (4c). Go up a short, very smooth wall to reach the groove. Follow the groove until it becomes steep, when it is possible to make a long step to the rib on the left, which leads to the belay on Rake End Wall.
2 35 feet (5a). Move round the bulge on the right and round the corner to a shallow and very steep scoop, which leads to a

junction with Rake End Wall. An exposed pitch.

3 70 feet (4c). Climb directly up the wall behind the ledge, then round the rib on the left into a steep groove. Continue up this groove to the terrace in Rake End Chimney. A cleaner way is to step down to the awkward move on pitch 3 of Rake End Wall.

Variation Finish 100 feet

3a 100 feet (5a). Go up for 30 feet to a bilberry-filled groove. Climb the groove in the middle of the wall on the left, until scrambling leads to Rake End Chimney.

*The Rib Pitch 120 feet Very severe (hard)

The right wall of Rake End Chimney drops back for 20 feet or so, forming a terrace. The left-hand rib remains, standing out boldly in isolation and giving a splendid pitch, steep and exposed. An excellent finish to either Rake End Wall or By-pass Route. Start from the final stance of Rake End Wall.

1 120 feet (4c). Make an upward traverse left to the rib and climb it to the top.

*The Bracken-clock 340 feet Extremely severe (E2)

Climbs the steep, smooth walls between By-pass Route and Stoat's Crack, avoiding the main steepness by an open groove on the right. These clean and open walls are attractively placed on the crag and, although the climb lacks a definite line, it is nevertheless very good and technically hard. Start a few yards left of the foot of the buttress.

1 60 feet (5a). Follow a shallow groove, past a difficult bulge to the right end of a ledge. Belay at the left end.

2 45 feet (5c). Climb directly up the smooth slabs with difficulty, to reach a traverse line. Step left to belay.

3 70 feet (5b). Traverse to the right for about 12 feet to a tiny platform on the edge of the smooth slabs. Climb directly above this platform, over an awkward bulge, then go up to the right into an open groove overlooking Stoat's Crack. Climb this to a ledge below a smooth little scoop.

4 80 feet (4a). Go up the scoop (as for Stoat's Crack) and walk to the right end of the ledge above. Follow slabs and ledges, trending right to a ledge below the final pitch of Stoat's Crack.

6 85 feet. Finish up the pleasant rib about 20 feet to the left.

Stickle Grooves 340 feet Very severe (hard)

Takes the front of the buttress direct, crossing Stoat's Crack low down and turning the midway overhangs on the right. The first wall is steep and strenuous and the upper pitches are by no means easy. Start up the smooth-looking wall on the left of Stoat's Crack, a few feet left of a shallow V-groove in the toe of the buttress.

1 70 feet (5a). Climb up to the right for 20 feet to below an overhang (or climb the V-groove direct to the same point). Go left for a few feet, past a flake, before climbing steeply up and back right above the overhang, to gain a shallow slanting groove. (This section is the crux.) Follow the groove to a good ledge (junction with Stoat's Crack).

2 50 feet. Go up easily to the ledge above and make an ascending traverse right to a juniper ledge.

3 80 feet (4c). Traverse across the wall on the left into the bottom of a smooth, rightward-slanting groove. Move up to the left, out of the groove, into a shallow scoop and follow it, past a small ledge, to a better one below the overhangs. Peg belay.

4 140 feet (4c). Climb the little slab on the right and the overhanging chimney above (very exposed) to easier ground and another smaller chimney. Go up this and the easy slabs to the top.

Andromeda 310 feet Very severe (hard)

Really a variation start to Stickle Grooves but the size of the pitch gives it a measure of independence. Start from the top of Pitch 1 of Stoat's Crack.

1 90 feet (5a). Climb a delicate little scoop a few feet right of the crack, go over the bulge and enter the niche above. Make a rising traverse right until a short wall leads to an overhung quartz ledge. Stomach traverse this to an uncomfortable stance on the left.

The rightward slanting groove of pitch 3 of Stickle Grooves lies across the wall on the left. Continue up pitches 3 and 4 of Stickle Grooves.

Variation

3a 50 feet (4c). Climb the chimney/groove a few feet right of the overhanging chimney of Stickle Grooves. It is harder and looser than the normal way.

**Stoat's Crack   375 feet   Severe (hard)

A good honest mountaineering route, the easiest way up a very big area of steep rock. The crux is quite hard, bold and with a fair amount of exposure. Start at the foot of the buttress.

1 55 feet. Climb a grassy corner to a ledge, descend a little and walk along to the foot of the steep crack; or reach this point by climbing the grassy wall direct.

2 65 feet. Go up the crack for about 25 feet, break out left and ascend to a stance on the corner.

3 85 feet. Traverse to the groove on the left and follow this and the open corner above to a capacious overhung ledge.

4 80 feet. Step round to the left, along the grass terrace, and climb an open groove, finishing to the right. Traverse left along another ledge and go up easy ground until it is possible to move right to below a sweep of slabs. A more difficult and direct way can be made from the top of the open groove.

5 90 feet. Climb pleasant slabs, delicate at first, then a short wall and slabs lead leftwards to a huge detached block. 100 feet of scrambling finishes the climb.

A route has been worked out on the loose and vegetated buttress right of Stoat's Crack and Stickle Grooves. The place is not attractive and those who are interested are left to work out their own line. The standard is Very severe.

The East Wall

The cliff now turns through an angle of ninety degrees and becomes steep and impressive; this is The East Wall.

*Brain Damage   225 feet   Extremely severe (E3)

The series of grooves on the left-hand side of the East Wall marks the line of this very strenuous climb. A rather nasty first pitch leads to a steep and exciting finish up the bulging wall. Start by scrambling up grass to a large spike, below some black streaks coming down from an overlap.

1 75 feet (6a). Move up to a ledge on the left and climb the wall to below a downward pointing flake in the overlap. Step left under this, then go up with difficulty to the foot of a steep green groove, which leads to a ledge and peg belays.

2 150 feet (5c). Gain the steep groove above and climb it to a standing position on a sharp flake on the right wall. Move right, round the rib and climb a steep wall to a peg below the overhang. Pull round the bulge and go up steep rock above to where the angle eases.

Coma   160 feet   Extremely severe (E3)†
Impressive and sustained climbing up the wall right of Brain
Damage, unfortunately encroaching on Mother Courage. Start
at a large flake, right of Brain Damage.
1 80 feet (6a). Climb straight up to the overhang, surmount this
  with difficulty and continue rightwards to the ledge. Belay as
  for Brain Damage.
2 80 feet (5c). Step back right and pull over the overhang; then
  climb up to a good hold. Traverse right into Mother Courage
  and go up this to the peg. Step down and left and climb into a
  groove, which leads to the top.

*Mother Courage   150 feet   Extremely severe (E3)
A very steep and strenuous pitch up the wall right of Brain
Damage. Start 20 feet right of Brain Damage.
1 150 feet (5c). Climb the wall, left of the obvious dirty groove,
  to a narrow ledge just left of a holly. Climb strenuously up the
  wall above the short steep gangway on the left, to reach a
  flat hold. Continue directly to a bulge, pull over this rightwards,
  immediately stepping back left to the foot of a steep groove.
  Climb the groove, past a peg, and pull out right to a good hold.
  Go up, still steeply, but with less difficulty, to a rib which leads
  to the top.

Red Groove   150 feet   Extremely severe (E1)
The obvious red groove, right of Mother Courage, gives an
enjoyable and interesting climb. Start by scrambling up from the
foot of Brain Damage or by moving down from the top of the
first pitch of Hobson's Choice.
1 95 feet (5a). Climb easily up the wall for 15 feet to a juniper.
  Traverse left across the impending wall, pull up with difficulty
  to a higher line and step left into a niche. Climb up to the
  easier groove, which leads to a good ledge below the final pitch
  of Hobson's Choice.
2 45 feet (4c). Finish up the impending V-groove on superb
  rough rock.

Risus   155 feet   Extremely severe (E2)
The second pitch has a high level of technical interest; quite
difficult for the grade. Start as for Red Groove.
1 90 feet (5b). Climb the first 15 feet of Red Groove and continue
  up the overhanging groove, just right of a detached block at
  the start of the traverse of Red Groove. Climb the groove to a
  poor resting place where it fades out; step left and climb up to

a terrace, which leads right to a stout juniper belay on Hobson's Choice.

2 65 feet (5c). Climb the steep gangway, which slants right from the tree and pull over an awkward bulge to the ledge above. Go diagonally left to a small ledge with a peg at the foot of a groove. Follow this to the overhang and move left to some good holds, which lead to the top.

Kudos 150 feet Extremely severe (E2)

The final pitch gives steep climbing on good finger holds. Start as for Risus.

1 100 feet (5b). Follow Risus for about 20 feet until a line of holds leads left onto the wall between Risus and Red Groove. Go up the groove line above, taking the left hand branch, to reach the good ledge below the final pitch of Hobson's Choice.

2 50 feet (5c). Climb the wall to the right of the final pitch of Red Groove to finish at the same point as Risus.

Solstice 160 feet Extremely severe (E4) (1 pt. aid)†

The obvious traverse line between Risus and Eclipse. Start below pitch 2 of Risus.

1 80 feet (6a). Climb Risus, until a crack leads up right. Climb this and traverse right until below the pod (peg runner). Go down and right to a small spike (rest taken here); continue the traverse into the groove of Eclipse and move out right with difficulty to a large grass ledge (as for Eclipse).

2 80 feet (4c). Climb the stepped corner and the obvious groove to the top (as for Eclipse).

*Hobson's Choice 205 feet Severe (hard)

Follows the obvious ledge on the East Wall and takes the form of a traverse rising from right to left. It is the easiest route on the wall and covers some interesting ground. Start up the sweep of slab below the big grooves of Astra and Fallen Angel.

1 60 feet. Climb the slab by any one of several indefinite lines. The rock is quite good but protection is sparse. Belay on a good ledge.

2 35 feet. Climb the steep little wall on the left, with some difficulty, to a slab which leads to a stance below the impressive corner of Eclipse.

3 50 feet. Take the easiest line leftwards to a short chimney-crack, which leads to a good juniper ledge below the top pitch of Risus.

4 30 feet. Walk along the ledge to a stance below the top pitch of Red Groove.

5 30 feet. Climb the awkward square-cut chimney at the left end of the ledge.

*Eclipse 150 feet Extremely severe (E4)

The obvious open corner above pitch 2 of Hobson's Choice gives a sustained pitch with increasing difficulty. Start from the stance below the corner.

1 70 feet (6a). Climb the steep corner for 20 feet to a ledge on the right. Continue up the open corner with a very difficult series of moves, to reach the grass ledge on the right. Care is needed to protect the second.

2 80 feet (4c). Climb the stepped corner above and pull out right to gain the foot of an obvious groove which leads to the top.

***Astra 200 feet Extremely severe (E2)

The superb, slim groove in the rib, right of Eclipse is reached by a bold but delightful wall pitch. Altogether a magnificent climb, perhaps the best in the valley. Start from the stance below Eclipse.

1 70 feet (5b). Cross the narrow easy-angled slab on the right to reach a steep undercut wall. Climb across this with difficulty to a resting place by a flake. Step up and left, delicately, to a ledge below another steep wall. Move up and right and continue across the wall past a thin crack to reach hidden holds round the edge, which enable a fine little stance to be gained. All this is very exposed.

2 115 feet (4c). Climb the series of grooves, on superb rock, to a grass ledge without a belay. Continue up the awkward V-groove to a much bigger grass ledge.

3 15 feet. Finish up the short crack, which leads to easy scrambling.

Supernova 150 feet Extremely severe (E4)†

An eliminate on the main pitch of Astra.

1 70 feet (6a). Traverse right as for Astra to a thin crack in the wall. Climb this to the glacis and continue straight up the slim scoop in the wall left of Astra, to the belay on Eclipse.

2 80 feet (4c). Finish up the stepped corner of Eclipse.

***Fallen Angel 155 feet Extremely severe (E4)

A superb and technically demanding climb up the impressive pod-shaped groove. Start by traversing along grass, above the sweep of slab to a belay below and to the right of the groove.

1 155 feet (6a). Climb the wide crack leading into the pod. Go up the pod, over the bulge (crux) and continue to the top of the groove. Step right onto a slab and go up this to a good foothold (possible belay but probably better to continue). Follow the thin crack above for 20 feet and step right to where another crack leads diagonally right to a bollard on the arête. Move left and into a groove and climb it to the top.

Heartsong 100 feet Extremely severe (E3)†
The very steep, thin, crack right of Fallen Angel.
1 100 feet (6b). Climb the crack, very sustained, and make a
  difficult exit onto Fallen Angel.

Cascade 230 feet Very severe (hard)
The last stretch of clean rock lies just left of the chimney of
Bennison and takes the line of two steepening slabs, one above the
other. An excellent climb, lacking the fierceness of its more
intimidating companions but providing a fair taste of the problems
of the East Wall. Start at the foot of the sweep of slabs, as for
Hobson's Choice.
1 80 feet (4c). Step across the steep wall and pull round onto the
  belt of slabs. Go up the right-hand side of the slabs, almost
  overlooking the gully, to a grass ledge at the top. Continue up
  a 10-foot corner on the left to a good ledge below the first
  slab.
2 75 feet (4c). Climb the slab just right of the corner, until
  steepening rock forces a rightwards traverse for a few moves.
  Move up to a small ledge and climb a short wall to reach
  another ledge.
3 75 feet (4b). The bulging chimney above is filled with a huge
  cigar-shaped rock. Climb the crack on either side of the cigar
  to the top.

*Cascade Direct 80 feet Extremely severe (E2)
A most enjoyable pitch with sustained technical difficulties.
Start from a ledge at the foot of the fine corner and left of the
belay below the final pitch of Cascade.
1 80 feet (5c). Climb the corner (peg runner low down) to an
  exit left at the overhang. It is usual to avoid the very steep
  section at the peg by stepping right up a slab to a ledge and
  then traversing horizontally left into the corner.

*Startrek 220 feet Extremely severe (E2)
A girdle of the upper section of the East Wall which covers no
new ground, but links a number of excellent pitches and gives
some magnificent situations. Start as for Eclipse.
1 60 feet (5c). Climb the corner of Eclipse for 20 feet to a ledge
  on the right. Move right into Astra and cross the wall past
  the thin crack, to reach the fine little stance at the top of
  Astra's first pitch.
2 110 feet (5b). Climb the groove above the stance to a good
  spike and traverse right to the arête. Step right and go down a
  groove, until a couple of awkward moves lead onto the slab
  of Fallen Angel (possible stance). Follow the thin crack above

for 20 feet and step right to where another crack leads diagonally right to a bollard on the arête, which gives a good belay without a stance.

3 50 feet (4c). Swing down into Cascade Direct and traverse right to finish up Cascade.

Other girdle traverses have been made, moving leftwards from Hobson's Choice; they have not proved popular, possibly because they are very vegetated and the character of the crag does not lend itself to satisfactory traversing. The intrepid explorer is left to rediscover these ways.

Bennison's Chimney and **Gibson's Chimney** are the two final weaknesses of the East Wall, starting high up the scree gully. The former will be enjoyed only by the nerveless devotee of vertical grass climbing; the latter is less frightening but offers only 50 feet of climbing.

RAVEN CRAG (285065)

Raven Crag includes Middlefell Buttress, the original Raven Crag (now known as Raven Crag Buttress), both situated immediately above the Old Dungeon Ghyll Hotel, and East Raven, the line of low crags extending towards Stickle Barn The crags are easily reached by a marked path from the Old Hotel; this path has been constructed to minimise the serious erosion from which the hill-side has suffered.

Middlefell Buttress

The clean easy-angled buttress, left of Raven Crag Buttress, gives a fine classic climb, with harder and less distinguished routes on both flanks.

Armalite 80 feet Extremely severe (E2)
A poorly protected pitch on the gully wall left of Middlefell Buttress. Start by scrambling up the gully a short way to a sloping block, just beneath a vague crack.
1 80 feet (5c). Follow a vague line for 15 feet to a ledge on the left. Continue up the wall to a pocket, which enables a move right to be made to a short groove. Climb this and the wall above to finish.

Higher up the gully there is another short wall with a loose rib (Walk Tall, E2, 5c) and a groove on its left (D.G. Corner, Very severe (hard), 5b).

*Middlefell Buttress 250 feet Difficult
A popular and well-scratched route giving pleasant climbing. The first pitch is Severe but this can be avoided. Start at the lowest point of the buttress.
1 50 feet. Climb the highly polished and strenuous crack to a large stance. This can be avoided by scrambling up to the left of the buttress. There is also another strenuous crack on the right.
2 150 feet. Follow the left side of the buttress, without difficulty, to another comfortable stance.
3 50 feet. Start the wall above by traversing from either left or right; then go up a fairly steep section to the finishing balcony.

Further pitches can be found to extend the climb as desired.

Bradley's Damnation   140 feet   Very severe (hard)
Follows a shallow groove straight up the wall right of Middlefell
Buttress. Quite hard, with a poor stance and belays and some
doubtful rock. Start at a huge block a few yards right of Middlefell
Buttress.
1 30 feet. Ascend easily above the pinnacle to a small stance and
   dubious belays below a steep corner.
2 80 feet (5a). Climb the short bulging wall which bars access to
   the groove. Follow this, until a jug enables the rib on the left
   to be gained. After a few more feet the angle eases and it is
   possible to move up right across grassy slabs to a small ledge.
3 30 feet (4a). Climb the short steep wall to the top.

Mendes   155 feet   Very severe
Less serious than Bradley's Damnation and on better rock. The
line of the route is the wall of the corner, right of Bradley's
Damnation. Start a few yards right of the pinnacle on easy-
angled rock below a small overhang.
1 40 feet. Go up easily leftwards past the overhang to a shallow
   groove. Climb it to a stance and belay on the right.
2 85 feet (4c). Traverse right for a few feet and climb up on good
   holds until a pull up left gives access to easier-angled rock.
   Continue up to a ledge and belays.
3 30 feet (4a). Climb the short steep wall to the top.

The Gamekeeper   125 feet   Very severe (hard)
Start about 10 feet right of Mendes, beyond a shallow corner.
1 100 feet (5b). Climb straight up until level with a shallow groove,
   a few feet to the left. Move awkwardly right; then follow the
   vegetated groove past the left end of a grassy bay to the foot
   of a groove, at the right end of the Mendes ledge.
2 25 feet. Climb the groove to the top.

Mendes Traverse (150 feet, Very severe (hard), 5a), is a very
strenuous route on doubtful rock, which starts at the right end
of the wall at a short groove and follows a traverse line from the
top of the groove into Mendes.

Raven Crag Buttress

Raven Crag Buttress is separated from Middlefell Buttress by an open gully (Raven Gully) and is bounded on its right by the Amphitheatre. It is steep, particularly in the centre, where there is an impressive line of overhangs; the rock is generally very good.

A rapid descent is afforded by a large grass shelf (Oak-tree Terrace), which gives easy access to the Amphitheatre from the upper right section of the crag. The terrace is reached from the top by a short descent over some large split blocks (the last pitch of Savernake).

Evening Wall 155 feet Severe
Start from Raven Gully about 20 feet to the left of the pinnacle belay at the top of the first pitch of Oak-tree Wall.
1 35 feet. Ascend for 15 feet until the wall steepens, when a traverse right can be made into a shallow corner. Step right and move up to a small stance and belay on the second pitch of Oak-tree Wall.
2 50 feet. Climb 10 feet to a ledge, traverse left and then go straight up to a bulge. Step up and traverse left again to an ash-tree.
3 70 feet. Move right onto the arête which leads to the top on good holds.

Evening Oak Variations 140 feet Very severe
Start a few feet left of Evening Wall.
1 70 feet (4c). Ascend slabs leftwards into a groove; follow this with increasing difficulty to the overhang. Move left and pull up to easier ground which leads, still steeply, to a ledge.
2 70 feet (4b). Move right and climb a shallow chimney through the overhangs to easier rocks, which lead to the top.

Oak-tree Wall 145 feet Severe (mild)
Start to the left of, and 40 feet higher than, the Original Route just below a prominent oak.
1 45 feet. Climb a short crack to the roots of the oak, move out right onto the wall and go up to a large ledge, with a pinnacle at its left end.
2 55 feet. Ascend the rib behind the belay to a small ledge below a bulging wall, where an overhung gangway leads up right to a small stance.
3 45 feet. Move up and slightly right to a ledge below a bulge, go up to the bulge, and turn it on its left by way of a shallow scoop.

*The Original Route   200 feet   Severe (mild)

A pleasant and well-marked route. Start at the lowest point of the left section of the buttress.

1 40 feet. Ascend slightly left, up a miniature gully, to a ledge.
2 50 feet. Follow a steep ridge to a ledge, which leads left to the pinnacle belay on Oak-tree Wall.
3 45 feet. Step back right and climb the steep wall above, trending slightly right, to a group of ledges.
4 65 feet. Go straight up for 15 feet, then move left to a ledge under a bulge. Step left along the ledge and climb a steep section, which gives access to an easy finish.

*Holly-tree Traverse   150 feet   Very difficult

An interesting, if somewhat rambling route. Start by scrambling up to the pinnacle belay on Oak-tree Wall from the foot of Raven Gully.

1 75 feet. Follow the ridge above the belay for 10 feet until it is possible to make an awkward traverse right to a sentry box on The Original Route (possible belay). Continue traversing rightwards to a conspicuous holly.
2 75 feet. Climb the rib to the right of a groove and traverse to a ledge below a right-angled corner. Finish up this on good holds.

Variation

2a 70 feet. Climb the groove to a small oak, move left onto the rib and finish up this, working slightly leftwards to finish.

Nadir   155 feet   Very severe

Pleasant enough, with one or two interesting moves.

1 40 feet (4b). Climb a delicate little rib, a few feet right of Oak-tree Wall to the good ledge.
2 115 feet (4c). Move rightwards along the ledge until it is possible to pull up awkwardly to a flake. Step right into a steep flake crack, climb steeply up to Holly-tree Traverse and continue directly to the top.

*Holly-tree Direct   190 feet   Very severe

An attractive climb which requires the delicate touch. The route takes one of the best lines on the crag—the long groove leading directly to the holly. Start just right of The Original Route, and scramble up 30 feet to a good ledge below a steep corner crack.

1 45 feet (4b). Climb the crack for about 30 feet until it is possible to move out right to the terrace below the groove.
2 70 feet (4c). Climb up onto a whitish slab on the left of the groove, and gain the recess in the groove above by a short

delicate traverse across the smooth rib. Pull out to the right
and climb up to a resting place. Continue up the groove,
steep and delicate at first, then easing, to reach the holly.
3 75 feet (4c). Step out left from a point a few feet above the
holly and climb the left rib of the groove.

Variation   Very severe (hard)
2a 60 feet (5b). Climb directly up to the groove; short, very
strenuous and poorly protected.

The groove right of Holly-tree Direct has been climbed.

**Trilogy   100 feet   Extremely severe (E4)
The great overhung corner which marks the left edge of the
central wall. An exciting pitch, steep and very strenuous. There
are fifteen pegs in place but many are of dubious worth. Start by
scrambling up to the ledge below the corner.
1 100 feet (6a). Climb the corner to a resting place below the
large overhang. Pull over this and continue directly to the top.

*Pluto   225 feet   Very severe (hard)
A convenient way of linking three basically independent pitches.
Individually the pitches are good and together they form a varied
and interesting way up the crag. A curving overhung break leads
rightwards from the foot of Trilogy; this is the second pitch. The
first pitch, a steep crack, leads up to the left end of this break.
Start at the foot of the crack.
1 50 feet (4c). Climb the crack to a good stance and belay.
2 90 feet (4b). Step right across the wall and climb up to the
overhung break. Follow this rightwards until an awkward
move across a groove leads to a comfortable stance on Bilberry
Buttress.
3 85 feet (5a). Step down onto the rib on the left and climb this
on small holds until it is possible to move right and up to a
traverse line (Bilberry Buttress). Follow this to an easy finish.

Green Groove Finish   90 feet   Extremely severe (E1)
The green groove left of pitch 3.
3a 90 feet (5b). Step down left into the obvious groove. Climb
this, with a move to the left to avoid a bulge at 25 feet.

R. 'n' S. Special   130 feet   Extremely severe (E4)
An excursion onto the wall right of Trilogy; good sustained
climbing but with little direction. Start below Trilogy.
1 130 feet (6a). Follow pitch 2 of Pluto until it is possible to pull
through the roof to enter a shallow scoop. Climb the wall to a
peg on the right. Traverse right to a good hold and ascend

directly to some sloping footholds. Step right (poor wire runner in place) then move up and right to better holds leading to the final roof (junction with Fine Time). Pull leftwards through the overhang on good holds to easy slabs and the top.

*Fine Time   150 feet   Extremely severe (E3)

A good pitch, taking the obvious crack through the overhangs, some 60 feet right of Trilogy. Steep scrambling leads to the foot of a rib just left of a patch of ivy.

1 150 feet (6b). Climb the rib to the roof. (An alternative approach is to climb Savernake and reverse the Pluto traverse for 20 feet.) Step right and climb the roof with great difficulty (peg runner) to reach a slanting crack. Follow this, then continue more easily to a second roof; turn this on the left to reach slabs and the top.

*Bilberry Buttress   230 feet   Very severe

A climb with a well-maintained standard of difficulty and a fine airy finish. Start at the lowest point of the right side of the crag.

1 65 feet (4b). Ascend easily to the foot of an obvious crack and climb this to a ledge and massive belays.

2 50 feet (4c). Climb the thin crack in the steep wall past a bulge to a magnificent finishing hold. Follow the ridge to a large sloping ledge.

3 115 feet (4b). Traverse the ledge to the right and climb a shallow crack for a few feet, until a few moves back left lead beneath a large detached block. Traverse leftwards beneath the overhang and continue horizontally across the green-groove. Make an exit left to easy ground after an upward step.

Savernake   255 feet   Severe (mild)

A similar line to Bilberry Buttress, but more circuitous and a great deal easier. Start at the same point as Bilberry Buttress.

1 85 feet. Ascend easily to the foot of the crack of Bilberry Buttress. Step down and round the corner on the right and climb the easy V-chimney to the ledge and massive belays on Bilberry Buttress.

2 70 feet. Walk down to the left, and then go up broken rocks in the corner, which gradually steepens to a fine exposed finish at the top of pitch 2 of Bilberry Buttress.

3 50 feet. Traverse the sloping ledge to the right end, and climb the broken corner for about 5 feet, until a step left can be made into a dirty scoop; then climb up over the detached block and continue to a large ledge and fine oak belay (Oak-tree Terrace).

4 50 feet. Walk to the right and finish over large blocks.

Nutcracker Cleft　220 feet　Very severe (hard)

A strenuous climb, similar to Kneewrecker Chimney but more contrived. Start up the big overhanging cleft on the right of Savernake.

1　80 feet (5a). Avoid the lower section by a short traverse from the right. From the tree, climb up to the overhang and pull out onto a glacis on the right. Follow the short steep crack in the corner and continue to a small slab, where the difficulties diminish. Move right and ascend easier angled rock to a ledge.

2　65 feet (4b). Climb up easily, then more steeply to a ledge; move right to belay below a bulging chimney-crack.

3　35 feet (4b). Turn the overhang by a short traverse left; then move back right into the chimney and follow it to the Split Blocks.

*Revelation　165 feet　Severe

A pleasant route up the prominent buttress on the right-hand face of the crag, bounded on the right in its upper section by an open chimney. Start at the foot of the buttress.

1　40 feet. Follow the buttress on small holds to a good ledge below an overhanging wall.

2　50 feet. Climb the short strenuous crack in the wall; continue past a small ledge and over a projecting nose to a sloping stance just left of Kneewrecker Chimney.

3　75 feet. Continue straight up over bulging rocks to Oak-tree Terrace. Either walk off, or finish up the blocks behind the tree, as for Savernake.

Kneewrecker Chimney　125 feet　Very severe (hard)

A strenuous gymnastic climb with an intimidating final pitch. Start from the oak a short way to the right of pitch 2 of Revelation.

1　40 feet (4b). Ascend the wall on the left of the tree until an entry can be made into an open scoop which leads to a sloping ledge.

2　50 feet (4b). Step back to the right and climb a strenuous crack to Oak-tree Terrace.

3　35 feet (5a). Climb the overhanging V-chimney behind the oak to a tiny ledge. Step up, and escape round the corner to the left on good holds, which lead to easier ground and the top.

*Raven Girdle   320 feet   Severe

A left to right traverse providing pleasant climbing and airy situations. Start from Raven Gully about 20 feet to the left of the pinnacle belay at the top of the first pitch of Oak-tree Wall.

1 35 feet. Ascend for 15 feet until the wall steepens, when a traverse can be made into a shallow corner. Step right, and move up to a small stance and belay on the second pitch of Oak-tree Wall (pitch 1 Evening Wall).

2 45 feet. Follow the overhung gangway of Oak-tree Wall, rightwards to a small stance.

3 80 feet. Traverse right making for the prominent ledge on the skyline. From the ledge, descend to a gnarled tree and cross the wall on the right to a ledge below a right-angled corner (Holly-tree Traverse).

4 35 feet. Climb down to a delightfully exposed slab and traverse rightwards across it to a ledge.

5 75 feet. Descend a little and traverse right, to an incipient gully; move down again for a few feet and continue the traverse up to the right to a ledge. Follow the ledge to its end, and step down to belay behind a pinnacle.

6 30 feet. Climb a little slab and continue the traverse to Oak-tree Terrace.

7 20 feet. Finish behind the split blocks as for Savernake.

Muscle Crack is the steep and thin crack round the corner to the right of the last pitch of Kneewrecker Chimney. It gives a difficult and unattractive little climb. (Very severe (hard).)

Bounding the buttress, high on its right, is a grassy bay (The Amphitheatre), the walls of which provide the following climbs:

Jaundice (185 feet, Severe) is a thoroughly unattractive route up the overgrown rocks on the left of Bluebell Gully.

Bluebell Gully   150 feet   Severe

The open grassy gully left of the prominent rock pinnacle. The climbing is better than the appearance suggests. Start at the foot of the gully.

1 50 feet. Climb the gully to a grassy corner.

2 100 feet. Continue up the gully for a few feet and make an awkward traverse onto the wall on the right; climb this to a ledge. Continue above the ledge until it is possible to step into the gully on the left, which leads to the top.

Bluebell Arête 145 feet Severe

Follows the steep arête between Bluebell Gully and Centipede. Start about 10 feet right of Bluebell Gully.

1 50 feet. Climb into a groove on the right and follow it for a few feet until it is possible to climb the steep right wall to the level of a rowan, when a traverse left can be made to the arête. Climb this to a small stance.

2 95 feet. Continue up the steep edge of the arête to the ledge on the final pitch of Bluebell Gully. Finish up this.

*Centipede 300 feet Severe

A very pleasant route. Start to the right of, and lower than, Bluebell Gully below the prominent pinnacle.

1 60 feet. Climb the steep rib, until a traverse can be made to a crack on the left. Follow this to a good ledge.

2 50 feet. Climb the steep slabs and turn the overhang on the left. Go up to a stance below a crack.

3 50 feet. Step down a few feet and traverse across the wall on the right to join the arête at a small ledge immediately above the overhang. Follow the arête to a good ledge.

4 140 feet. Continue up the ridge by a series of steps, some of which are rather awkward.

Variation

The overhang on pitch 2 can be climbed direct (E1, 5b).

Right of Centipede, there is a large grassy terrace. **Confidence** (160 feet Severe) takes a blunt arête above this terrace; any one of three ribs below give a first pitch.

The next two climbs are situated on a small broken-looking buttress some 100 yards right of the Amphitheatre.

Hot Pot (75 feet Very severe) follows a rib on the left side of the buttress.

Stewpot 110 feet Severe

Start at the lowest point of the buttress.

1 40 feet. Climb up broken rocks, over a large detached block and up a slab to a ledge.

2 35 feet. Climb a small slab and then broken rocks to another ledge with a pinnacle on the left.

3 35 feet. Climb onto the pinnacle and finish up the wall to the right. (The finishing move is much harder than the rest of the climb.)

Variation

3a 35 feet. Climb a short crack down to the right near the arête; slightly harder than the normal way.

East Raven

The buttresses of East Raven are generally smooth with very few features, with the exception of a deeply-cut right-angled gully, containing a large holly, about halfway along, and a big unpleasant-looking overhanging cleft at about the threequarter mark; these break the crag up and serve as convenient markers.

Mamba   70 feet   Severe (mild)
A steep and pleasant wall about 15 feet from the left-end. An awkward mantelshelf at 40 feet is the crux.

Jingo   60 feet   Very severe (mild)
Start at the same point as Speckled Band and climb directly up the wall, pulling up left at half-height.

Speckled Band   60 feet   Very difficult
An obvious line slanting up to the right about 8 yards right of Mamba. A direct start is round the corner on the right (Very severe).

Jungle Wall   80 feet   Severe (hard)
A large oak growing on a ledge 30 feet up marks the route. Start below the tree.
1 50 feet. Climb up and across to the right to a large sloping ledge and then move back left to the tree.
2 30 feet. Climb the steep, fist-wide crack on the right to the top of the pinnacle; step right, and finish up the gully.

Festerday   120 feet   Very severe (hard)
The steep crack in the wall left of Rowan-tree Groove.
1 120 feet (5a). Go directly up the wall to the crack, which is strenuous for the first 30 feet.

Rowan-tree Groove   120 feet   Very severe
The groove, starting halfway up the crag and topped by overhangs; a good climb. Start just left of the obvious V-groove of Casket, which lies about 5 yards left of the deep right-angled gully.
1 60 feet (4a). Climb the steep wall to a blunt pinnacle; step up and round the corner on the left, and traverse diagonally left to belay about 5 feet below and right of the crack on Jungle Wall.
2 60 feet (4b). Move back right and enter the groove with difficulty. Climb to the overhang and traverse right to the rib which leads to the top.

Ramrod   100 feet   Very severe
The slim groove right of Rowan-tree Groove; clean and direct.
Start just right of Rowan-tree Groove.
1 100 feet (4c). Climb up to the blunt pinnacle and continue up
the left hand rib of the smooth little V-groove to the overhangs
below the slim groove. Follow this to the top.

Casket   105 feet   Very severe
The obvious V-groove 5 yards left of the deep right-angled
gully.
1 105 feet (4c). Climb the groove, past a tree to easy ground.

The Chopper   100 feet   Very severe (hard)
The steep wall right of Casket is clean and attractive, but the
route is very contrived.
1 100 feet (5a). Climb the wall, the crux being a rising traverse
left into Casket.

Baskerville   100 feet   Very severe (mild)
The steep rib immediately left of the gully gives a pleasant pitch.
1 100 feet (4b). Gain a small ledge at 20 feet, either by the direct
ascent of a groove, or by traversing in from the left. Follow the
rib on the right to the top.

Ornithology   85 feet   Severe
The right wall of the gully.
1 85 feet. Follow a steep little rib to the right end of a ledge, at
30 feet, and continue up the wall, which gradually eases towards
the top.

Shizen Groove   100 feet   Very severe (mild)
A pleasant climb up the steep wall right of Ornithology.
1 100 feet (4b). Climb the shallow groove which is easier than it
looks.

Joker's Slab   110 feet   Extremely severe (E1)
Start as for Shizen Groove.
1 110 feet (5a). Climb to just below the overhang, move right into
another groove, trending rightwards over two bulges, and
follow a traverse line leading right. Move up and right and then
back left to finish.

Brown Trousers   100 feet   Very severe (hard)
Quite a good route. Start at a short slab a few feet right of the
overhanging cleft.
1 100 feet (5a). Climb the slab to the left end of the overhangs.
Pull up, and traverse right above the overhangs to a blunt
rib, which leads to the top.

Sign of Four   95 feet   Very severe
Start 20 yards to the right of the overhanging cleft, at a corner.
1 95 feet (4c). Climb the corner to a holly nestling beneath the
   overhang. Traverse awkwardly right onto the front of the
   buttress, and after a delicate step, climb directly to the top.

Watson Wall   100 feet   Severe (hard)
The blunt rib a few yards right of Sign of Four.
1 100 feet. Climb past the overhang and traverse left to a shallow
   niche (or climb to this direct; considerably more difficult).
   Ascend diagonally right to a small ledge on the rib, which
   leads, trending left, to the top.

Subsidiary Ridge   95 feet   Very difficult
Start about 6 feet left of the lowest point of the small subsidiary
buttress, which lies about 30 feet right of Watson Wall.
1 95 feet. Ascend to a ledge, step up and left and climb to the
   top, keeping a few feet left of the crest all the way.

Far East Raven

Some two or three hundred yards nearer to Stickle Barn, and
lower down the fellside, is another short, steep buttress known as
Far East Raven.

The arête at the extreme left end of the buttress gives a short
climb (**Pianissimo**, 60 feet, Severe).

The Shroud   75 feet   Very severe (hard)
1 75 feet (5a). Follow the groove which slants to the right to a
   line of overhangs at 40 feet; step back right and trend left to a
   dirty finish.

Jericho Wall   115 feet   Very severe (hard)
Start about 20 yards from the left end of the crag at a short,
rightward-slanting glacis.
1 65 feet (4a). Climb the glacis and continue directly upwards,
   past a holly, to belay at a second holly below a yellow bulge.
2 50 feet (5b). Follow the curving crack left to a ledge; from a
   standing position on some spikes, pull over the overhang and
   swing left onto a steep and exposed wall. Climb this to the top.

Babylon 105 feet Extremely severe (E1)
A difficult climb with an atmosphere unusual for such a small
crag. Start at the foot of a cracked rib, just left of a vegetated
corner.
1 55 feet (4a). Climb straight up through the trees until it is
    possible to step right to a stance, below a curving break
    leading through the overhangs.
2 50 feet (5b). Follow the break, which gives sustained climbing
    to the very end.

The stretch of steep rubbishy rock, topped by an overhang, has
a number of pitches, but none of these has an exit, except for
a piton route across the overhang itself.

Nineveh 95 feet Very severe
Start at a groove which marks the right end of the rubbishy rock.
1 40 feet (4b). Climb the groove to the second of two niches,
    then break out right onto a slab which leads to a ledge and
    holly-tree belay.
2 55 feet (4b). Follow the rib on the left and finish up a slab,
    slanting right.

Samarkand 115 feet Very severe (hard)
Start directly below the holly on Ninevah.
1 45 feet (4b). Climb the wall to the holly.
2 70 feet (5b). Ascend the shallow groove to a peg runner and
    make a very difficult exit left. Continue delicately leftwards for
    a few feet and then move up to a small ledge. Step back right
    above the overhangs and finish up the wall above.

The steep groove right of Samarkand has been climbed. It is a
very difficult but not particularly attractive problem (100 feet,
Extremely severe E2).

Damascus 145 feet Very severe
The line of square-cut grooves gives a climb of character and
shape. Start just left of the lowest point of the buttress.
1 65 feet (4c). Go up to the first groove and climb it to a stance
    below the next corner.
2 80 feet (4b). Climb the corner and pull out on the right to easy
    slabs. Step round a little rib on the left into the last and
    smallest groove. Climb this, still with difficulty, to an exit on
    the left and an easy finish.

Peascod's Route   130 feet   Very severe (mild)
Start at the lowest point of the crag on the right-hand side.
1 60 feet (4b). Go up to the higher of two ledges below a bulge.
   Work round the nose on the right and pull up onto a sloping
   ledge.
2 70 feet (4b). Climb up to a triangular ledge below a steep
   right-angled corner. Follow this to the overhang, step left
   under it and finish up a small slab.

Variation   75 feet   Severe (hard)
1a 75 feet. Climb up to the first groove of Damascus, move right
   to a steep gangway and follow this to the triangular ledge
   below the right-angled corner.

Girdle Traverse   305 feet   Very severe
An enjoyable expedition, sustained at Severe level, with one or
two short sections a little harder. Eminently suitable for days
when higher cliffs are weather bound. Start as for Pianissimo, at
the left end of the crag.
1 45 feet (4b). Climb through the tree to a small ledge; then move
   up to the arête on the right. Belay a few feet higher.
2 65 feet (4b). Follow the obvious line right and after a few feet
   move down a little. Make a long stride across an open groove
   to good holds which lead to a stance at the holly on Jericho
   Wall.
3 20 feet. Move round the corner to another tree belay.
4 40 feet (4b). Step down and cross the slab to yet another tree
   belay.
5 25 feet (4b). Descend the rib and step right to a ledge and holly
   belay.
6 35 feet (4a). Go through the trees and traverse across and up
   slightly to a good ledge below the steep corner crack of
   Damascus.
7 75 feet (4b). Climb the crack, until a short slab leads right to
   the triangular ledge on Peascod's Route. Climb the right-
   angled corner to the overhang and traverse right to an awkward
   finish.

BOWFELL

The climbs on Bowfell are most comfortably reached from Langdale by way of the Three Tarns track leading up the Band. The track keeps to the left of the ridge and overlooks Oxendale and Hell Ghyll. After the fairly steep preliminary section, the Band levels out rather and the track veers to the right, passing above Neckband crag on the Mickleden side. When the ridge running up to Bowfell is reached, the track, which now turns left, is quitted and the ridge itself is ascended until a cairn on a patch of red scree indicates the next turning. From here an undulating path reminiscent of the High Level Route to Pillar Rock leads to the right, below a line of outcrops, passes underneath Flat Crags and the Cambridge Crag, and drops over a scree shoot to the foot of Bowfell Buttress.

The Buttress can be reached from Mickleden either by taking a diagonal line up Green Tongue, which is about halfway up the valley, or by ascending the first section of Rossett Ghyll and then working back leftwards over rough ground straight for the crag. The Band route will be thought easier.

The main climbs on Bowfell are situated on three separate crags in a rough semi-circle towards the summit of the mountain. The Neckband Crag is smaller, lower and adds climbing of a very different character to the group. Of the three upper crags, the first reached from Langdale is Flat Crags, facing almost due north, and easily recognisable from its name. The rock is of a peculiar formation, consisting of steep, smooth walls separated by a series of flat gangways running upwards from right to left, the topmost one leading easily to the main ridge.

From the right-hand end of this highest gangway rises the Cambridge Crag, facing north east, and, like both Flat Crags and Bowfell Buttress, having a sharp-cut obtuse-angled base. The rock formation is entirely different from Flat Crags and consists of numerous sharp-topped broken ridges, separated by short grooves and cracks. The right-hand and steepest section is known as North Buttress; its prominent features are three big grooves, roughly in the middle.

Beyond this crag comes a wide fan-shaped scree shoot running down from the main ridge and then, facing east, the imposing Bowfell Buttress. The Buttress has a well-marked nose dividing it into two different faces. On the left, the end-on strata form ridges and cracks similar to the Cambridge Crag. On the right the cleavage face offers an almost unbroken slab, from top to bottom.

The crag appears from below to lie against the fell-side. In actual fact it is cut off behind by a cleft, which runs south, over broken rock and scree, into the fan-shaped scree shoot from the main ridge, to give an easy means of descent, and north to join North Gully, which bounds the buttress on its northern side. In winter, this gives a steep snow slope with a steep pitch near the bottom, which can be avoided by an excursion up the fellside on the right. The climbs are described from left to right.

Flat Crags (245069)

The climbs start from the large sloping gangway which runs up leftwards under the crag.

Mary Ann 140 feet Very difficult
An attractive little route up a belt of slabs to the left of the steepest part of the crag. Start just right of a large flake, some 20 feet right of a mossy cave, about three quarters of the way up the gangway.
1 75 feet. Climb a short crack, step right to another crack and follow this to a line of overhangs. Traverse left below these and go up into a slabby bay.
2 65 feet. Go up a short crack, make a rising traverse left across the slabby wall and finish steeply on good holds.

Solaris 120 feet Extremely severe (E2)
Start about 50 yards up the gangway at an easy-angled slab below a big open corner (Flat Crag Corner). The climb takes the obvious groove left of this corner; a pleasant route.
1 120 feet (5c). Scramble up to the groove and climb it, eventually moving right to gain the left end of a large ledge. Swing down and across left, to climb the left arête of the groove to easy slabs.

Slowburn 120 feet Extremely severe (E1)
The wall left of Flat Crag Corner. Start at the foot of that climb.
1 120 feet (5b). Scramble up for a few feet and climb the wall on the left. Trend rightwards and then go left to a ledge on the arête. Follow the edge of the wall up and right to easy slabs leading to the top.

Flat Crag Corner 155 feet Very severe
A good climb up the big open corner above an easy-angled slab, about 50 yards up the ramp. Start at the foot of the slab.
1 80 feet. Climb easily up to the corner.
2 75 feet (4c). Climb the corner, past a ledge to a short finishing chimney with a doubtful chockstone.

B.B. Corner 130 feet Very severe (hard)
A line of corners just to the right of Flat Crag Corner. Start in a steep groove, which leads up to the right end of the ledge on pitch 2 of Flat Crag Corner.
1 85 feet (5a). Move up left of the groove and then move back right and climb the right wall for a few feet; step back into the main corner, which leads to the ledge.
2 45 feet (5a). Climb the corner, past a difficult bulge to the top.

Flat Iron Wall 140 feet Extremely severe (E1)
A bold, open route up the wrinkled wall right of B.B. Corner. Start at the foot of that climb.
1 75 feet (5a). Make a rising traverse to gain a small grass ledge on the right. Step right again and go directly up the wall to a ledge on the arête; move up to a stance on the larger ledge above.
2 65 feet (5a). Climb three, successive, little corners on the left to finish.

Fastburn 120 feet Extremely severe (E1)
A direct line up Flat Iron Wall. Start at a crack, 4 yards right of B.B. Corner.
1 120 feet (5b). Climb the crack to a grass ledge (junction with Flat Iron Wall). Continue up the wall, trending left to the obvious crack; climb this, moving out right at the top. Finish up a line of ledges leading left.

The prominent groove, right of Flat Iron Wall, has only been reached by the use of several slings on the overhanging wall, which guards access to it.

Ataxia 160 feet Extremely severe (E4)†
The overhanging crack at the right hand side of the crag. Start 20 feet up the access ramp below a roof crack.
1 80 feet (6b). Climb the crack to a ledge out on the right. Move left and follow the crack and groove above, moving out left to a small ledge.
2 80 feet (4c). The slabs above, trending leftwards.

Flat Crags Climb   150 feet   Severe

A line up the right end of the crag, escapable by walking right from any stance. Start below a steep slab.

1 45 feet. Climb the slab and step left to a recess at 20 feet. Traverse right and upwards to a good ledge.
2 55 feet. Traverse left along the ledge for 20 feet, round an awkward corner; then go up to a large terrace.
3 50 feet. Enter a steep chimney via a groove on the left and finish up the smooth slab on the left.

Cambridge Crag (245069)

Borstal Buttress   230 feet   Severe

A good first pitch but the succeeding ones can be avoided. Start left of a steep wall in a corner, about 60 yards above and to the left of the spring at the foot of the crag.

1 75 feet. Traverse right across the wall; then go straight up (loose holds near the finish require care).
2 45 feet. Climb the rib on the right and cross a slab to a crevasse and boulders.
3 65 feet. Continue up to the left by several small chimneys, the last loose one of which may be avoided on the right.
4 45 feet. Cross the rib on the right and descend to a V-corner. Go up a thin groove running left and scramble to the top.

The Cambridge Climb   250 feet   Difficult (hard)

An interesting route. Start just to the left of the spring at the foot of a broad slab sloping upwards to the right.

1 35 feet. Climb the slab to the foot of a corner.
2 30 feet. Step round the edge on the right and go up to a ledge.
3 45 feet. Traverse left to the second of two niches and go up past a sharp flake to a grassy corner.
4 50 feet. Ascend the pleasant chimney to a ledge on the right.
5 35 feet. Step back into the chimney and go up to a large terrace.
6 55 feet. Follow the large steps up to the right to the final balcony. Finish by scrambling up the dirty gully on the right.

North Buttress (245069)

The steep buttress above and to the right of Cambridge Crag. The main features of the crag are three open grooves.·

Siamese Chimneys (270 feet Severe), a rather unsatisfactory route, follows two steep, clean chimneys, separated by grass, and situated on the left side of the buttress.

Gnomon 230 feet Very severe (hard)

The left, and most broken, of the three big grooves offers steep and interesting climbing, in spite of its appearance. Start from the ledge below the right hand groove and scramble along ledges to a large spike belay below twin cracks.

1 95 feet (5b). Ascend the crack in the corner to a niche, make a long stride left and climb a steep little wall to another niche. Move up to a little ledge on the left rib, with difficulty; swing back into the groove and go up to a good ledge. Continue straight up to a grassy terrace.

2 60 feet. Scramble up to below the final buttress.

3 75 feet (4b). Finish up a line of holds leading rightwards.

Mindbender 100 feet Extremely severe (E2)

The central groove, which gives a good pitch. Start from the ledge, as for Gnomon, and scramble across to the foot of the groove.

1 100 feet (5b). Climb the groove, past a difficult bulge to easier ground. Finish by scrambling.

The Gibli 180 feet Very severe (hard)

Scrappy and contrived, but includes some hard climbing. Start as for Sword of Damocles.

1 20 feet (4c). From the small pinnacle at the left end of the ledge, pull into a short steep crack and climb it to a stance behind a huge pinnacle.

2 30 feet (5b). Climb the left one of twin V-grooves. Belay up on the right, as for Sword of Damocles.

3 80 feet. Follow the cracked wall, pleasantly, to a ledge on the arête and continue easily up the grassy gully to below a steep crack in the nose on the right.

4 50 feet (4c). Climb the crack, which overhangs at first, then move rightwards to the top.

*Sword of Damocles 180 feet Extremely severe (E1)

A fine, classic climb of considerable technical interest, which follows the right-hand, and largest, of the three grooves; alas, the Sword, which adorned the second pitch, is no longer with us. Start from a ledge, below and just left of the groove, at the foot of a prominent curved crack.

1 75 feet (4b). Enter a groove on the right by an upward traverse along the curved crack and go easily up to the foot of a groove behind a huge pinnacle. Climb the groove, until a long stride right can be made to gain a ledge on the edge of the buttress; go up a little until a traverse can be made across the groove to

a stance on the left wall.

2 45 feet (5b). Climb the groove, past an awkward bulge, to a small stance.

3 60 feet (5a). Climb the steep and impressive flake-crack to a resting place; continue up the crack, until a move right leads to easier climbing and the top.

Mindprobe 180 feet Extremely severe (E3)

The grooves in the arête to the right of Sword of Damocles give a bold and difficult climb. Start as for Sword of Damocles.

1 90 feet (5c). Climb a slabby groove to below two steep grooves. Go up the left hand one and make an awkward move into the right-hand one. At the top of this move left and climb the green, open groove to a peg runner. Continue up, with difficulty, to better holds and swing up right to a ledge.

2 90 feet (5b). Go across left to the foot of an overhanging corner which leads with difficulty to a pinnacle. Move up right to the arête and finish up this.

Scabbard 145 feet Very severe

A fairly direct line up the cliff just around the corner from Sword of Damocles; though short, it provides an interesting climb with a nice position. Start about 40 feet to the right of Sword of Damocles, at a thin crack.

1 65 feet (4c). Climb the thin crack to a long ledge and continue steeply to gain a shallow scoop, a few feet from the edge of the rib. Follow the scoop to a stance.

2 80 feet (4b). Go up the widening crack and finish up broken grooves.

Swastika 375 feet Very severe (hard)

A right to left girdle of North Buttress; rather contrived but enjoyable, clean and interesting, and including one of the best pitches on the cliff. Start as for Sword of Damocles.

1 35 feet (4c). Follow the upward-curving crack into the groove on the right; climb this for a few feet and then go back left behind an enormous pinnacle.

2 90 feet (4c). Move left, and drop down to a large sloping ledge below a smooth-looking groove. Swing down round the far edge and pull up into a niche. Traverse delicately left and go down and round to the left, to a grassy niche. Step down and continue to a larger grass ledge.

3 75 feet (5a). Move up and round the rib to reach a big white scoop, and go across to the corner on the far side. Step up across this corner and gain the front of the impressive pillar on the left. Step delicately up to reach a steep, sharply undercut

crack and follow it to some ledges.
4 90 feet. Climb up easily to the foot of a cracked wall.
5 85 feet (4c). Start at the left end of the wall and climb up to a pinnacle on the ridge at about 25 feet. Step right into a line of cracks and follow these to the top.

Bowfell Buttress (245069)

The Plaque Route 280 feet Difficult
A pleasant all-weather climb, with good belays, up the left edge of the buttress. Start from a large boulder, at the point where scree and grass meet at the foot of the crag.
1 40 feet. Go straight up to climb a difficult crack, or an easier scoop on the left, and follow easy rocks to a good belay.
2 40 feet. Climb the rib above to a small stance.
3 40 feet. Continue up a mossy groove and then a grass terrace.
4 30 feet. Ascend slabs diagonally rightwards to a ledge.
5 70 feet. Traverse right and go up a chimney; step onto the ridge on the right (where the Plaque is to be seen) and go up to a stance.
6 60 feet. Move right over easy slabs into a chimney which leads to the top.

Sinister Slabs 345 feet Severe (hard)
A pleasant if somewhat broken route, the second pitch being the most difficult. Start below a rib about 8 yards left of the lowest point of the buttress.
1 110 feet. Climb the rib for about 30 feet and move right over a block; work back left for 12 feet and then go straight up to a ledge. Climb the slanting chimney on the left to belay below an overhanging corner.
2 95 feet. Ascend a narrowing slab, slanting left; climb over some doubtful blocks and, after a few feet, go up to a rib on the right. Make a move or two up the rib and traverse right into a groove. After an awkward step, go out to a ledge on the right and step across to a good ledge.
3 80 feet. Climb first a chimney, then a gully, followed by a rib.
4 60 feet. Follow easy rock and then a crack in the steep rough slab to a flat ledge. Finish up the little wall above.

The Central Route 255 feet Severe (hard)

An interesting route of some difficulty. The climb starts 3 yards right of Bowfell Buttress, crosses this at the top of the first pitch and thereafter keeps to its left.

1 45 feet. Climb the broken groove to a stance at the top of the initial rib of Bowfell Buttress.

2 55 feet. Climb the overhanging chimney and its easier continuation to block belays.

3 65 feet. Step left from the belay and follow the easiest line up to a stance below a large block.

4 90 feet. Step onto the block and climb a thin groove, with increasing difficulty, to an awkward finish into a recess. Go up the steep rib on the right; then follow a slanting slab on the left and finish by scrambling.

Rubicon Groove 335 feet Extremely severe (E1)

A line of grooves, more or less directly above the start of Central Route. The crux involves some difficult and committing moves in an exposed position but the remainder of the climb is somewhat disappointing, though clean and on good rock. Start as for Central Route.

1 55 feet. Climb the shallow groove, step left and ascend to a stance below the overhang.·

2 60 feet (5b). Above on the left is a steep, deeply cut groove, undercut at its base. Go diagonally left under the overhang into a corner, which runs parallel to the groove and a few feet to its left. Climb the corner for a few feet until a traverse can be made across the right wall to a good hold on the rib. Continue right until the bed of the groove is reached and go up this to a stance.

3 120 feet (4c). Step back left across the groove and go diagonally left up steep slabs to the foot of two thin cracks. Climb these, and the chimney formed by their union, to a good ledge.

4 100 feet (4c). Follow the easy ridge to below the steep rough slab of Sinister Slabs. Move right and climb an awkward niche in the wall to the top.

***Bowfell Buttress** 350 feet Very difficult

A classic, high mountain route, the easiest way up an impressive buttress, giving climbing of considerable quality and interest. Start below a ridge, slightly left of the lowest point of the crag.

1 45 feet. Ascend the ridge to a good belay.

2 30 feet. Climb the short chimney on the right and go up easy ground to a terrace.

3 40 feet. Climb the steep wall above, moving diagonally left to a sentry box in a chimney.

4 60 feet. Follow the chimney for 40 feet and continue up easy ledges to a terrace sloping down to the right; walk along it for 25 feet to a crack on the right.

5 55 feet. Climb the awkward crack for 15 feet; then go up to the left to slabby rocks leading to a pinnacle belay.

6 60 feet. Move left for a few feet and ascend a groove leading into a chimney. Go up to a slab and continue up the wall above until a long stride left leads upwards to a platform and large belay.

7 60 feet. Step back to the right and follow a groove and its left branch to the finish.

Bowfell Buttress Eliminate   305 feet   Extremely severe (E1)
A fairly direct line, right of Bowfell Buttress, finishing up the big smooth wall at the top right corner. Interesting climbing but rather contrived. Start about 15 yards right of Bowfell Buttress.

1 45 feet. Go up steep slabs and finish by a groove on the right.

2 70 feet (4c). Climb the groove above direct to the belay below the awkward crack on Bowfell Buttress.

3 75 feet (4b). Climb the deep V-groove on the right to a ledge below a steep wall. Ascend the corner on the left for a few feet, before swinging back right onto the steep wall above the belay. Go up easier rock to a small niche on the left.

4 40 feet (5b). Ascend the smooth wall to a short, thin crack which leads to a narrow ledge.

5 75 feet (5b). Step right, and make some awkward moves right to the edge of the buttress. Climb a steep crack on the right to easier ground and the top.

Variation. Direct Finish

5a 50 feet (5b). Climb the obvious break through the overhangs to the summit.

Ledge and Groove   335 feet   Severe (mild)
A rambling route on the edge of the crag overlooking North Gully, which can be reached from several points on the climb by easy scrambling to the right. Start about 30 yards right of the lowest point of the crag and about 15 yards left of the gully.

1 55 feet. Ascend a short wall and groove to a large ledge; continue up a rib to another ledge and follow it to its right end.

2 70 feet. Go up a short wall, followed by a staircase to the right leading to a ledge below a small overhang. Move left on good holds for 15 feet and then go back right to a stance overlooking the gully.

3 40 feet. Step up, traverse right to a groove and go up it to a

sloping ledge. Follow this leftwards to the ridge which leads to a stance.

4 50 feet. Make a delicate traverse right (crux) and continue rightwards to a chimney; go up this to a ledge.

5 65 feet. Climb the groove on the right to a ledge and traverse left to the foot of a steep crack. Go up this for a few feet and make an awkward move onto a small ledge on the left, followed by a short but rather difficult ascent to a large terrace.

6 55 feet. Go diagonally left to a crack; climb this and the short wall above to finish.

Right-hand Wall 200 feet Very severe
An interesting route up the steep left bounding wall of North Gully; pleasant and exposed in its middle section. Start just above the steep pitch in the gully, at the foot of a conspicuous corner.

1 70 feet. Climb the corner to a ledge.

2 70 feet (4c). Traverse left across the wall on good flakes and go up a short crack to a ledge Continue delicately left up the wall to a small ledge and ascend a thin groove, with some difficulty, to good holds which lead to a ledge and large belay.

3 60 feet (4b). Start a few feet right of the belay and follow cracks to the top.

Right Wall Eliminate 200 feet Very severe (hard) (1 pt aid)†
The wall is followed from bottom left to top right. Start about 20 feet above the chockstone in North Gully, below a short rightward facing corner.

1 120 feet (5a). Go up to the corner, climb it to a quartz band and traverse right to a ledge. Ascend the crack from the right-hand end of the ledge and go up a bottomless groove to another ledge on the right.

2 40 feet (5a). Climb the crack on the right for 20 feet, step right and enter a second bottomless groove. Climb this, using a sling on a small quartz nodule, and step right to a spike.

3 40 feet (5a). Finish up the groove on the right.

Grey Corner 130 feet Severe (mild)
The smooth wall right of the upper half of Ledge and Groove is bounded on its right by a slabby corner. Start about two thirds of the way up North Gully, below the corner.

1 90 feet. Climb the groove and move out right to a ledge on the rib. Return to the corner and climb it on its left wall to a ledge. Follow a series of large holds, slanting left (awkward) and then go right to belay.

2 40 feet. Finish up the corner.

Grey Rib   155 feet   Severe (mild)
The right-hand rib of Grey Corner is clean and attractive but
in its upper half the difficulties are avoidable on the right.
1 65 feet. Follow the rib, more or less direct, to a good ledge.
2 90 feet. Continue up the rib, awkward at first, to the top.

Bowfell Buttress Girdle   500 feet   Very severe (mild)
A wandering route, much of it rather indefinite, but with a fine
finish. Start from a large boulder at the point where scree and
grass meet at the foot of the left end of the crag, as for Plaque
Route.
1 80 feet. Go straight up to climb a difficult crack, followed by
   easy rocks to a rib which leads to a stance (as for Plaque
   Route).
2 70 feet. Continue up the groove to a grassy terrace, traverse
   right, moving down to an obvious crevasse. Go up slightly,
   finishing with an awkward step round a rib. (Junction with
   Sinister Slabs.)
3 70 feet. Traverse right to a huge wedged block, forming part of
   the nose of the buttress; climb directly up the nose for 20 feet
   before continuing the traverse across to an embedded boulder.
4 50 feet. Climb the short wall diagonally from left to right to a
   junction with Bowfell Buttress.
5 40 feet. Move left for a few feet, ascend a groove leading into a
   chimney and go up to a slab with a flake belay.
6 130 feet (4c). Descend slightly rightwards to the foot of a
   chimney groove. Make a difficult step round the corner onto a
   steep slab. Traverse delicately across until an awkward move
   enables large holds to be reached. Continue right and climb
   the edge of the buttress for a few feet until it is possible to gain
   the thin groove of Right-hand Wall; go up this to a ledge.
7 60 feet (4b). Start a few feet right of the belay and follow cracks
   to the top (as for Right-hand Wall).

Neckband Crag (261061)

This is the small crag just below the summit of the Band on the
north-east side. The ascent of the Band, followed by a descent to
the foot of the crag, forms the easiest means of approach. A
small impressively steep crag, on which climbs have considerable
character. The place is very mossy; not suitable for wet weather
climbing. The climbs are described from right to left.
At the extreme right end, a steep little wall facing Bowfell
provides a hardish Severe pitch of about 60 feet.

The Neckband 205 feet Very difficult

A well-marked route up the prominent rib at the right end of the crag. Start at the foot of the rib.

1 95 feet. Follow the line of the rib past ledges and slabs.
2 110 feet. Continue up the same line to finish up a steep little corner.

Nectar 230 feet Very severe (mild)

After a hard start, difficulties rapidly diminish. Start about 12 yards left of The Neckband.

1 65 feet (4b). Go up a steep slab for a few feet to an open groove on the right; climb this until a move can be made onto the arête, which leads to a stance.
2 90 feet. Traverse left for 15 feet and climb a pleasant rib to a ledge. Continue up the short slab on the left and then a thin crack to a spike belay.
3 75 feet. Finish up the easy rocks above.

Flying Blind 200 feet Extremely severe (E3)†

The arête left of Nectar. Start just to its left.

1 80 feet (6a). Gain the arête from the left and climb it to a poor spike at 45 feet. Move right to a crack and go up this for a few feet to a doubtful block. Move immediately left to regain the arête; climb this and the easier ground above to a ledge.
2 120 feet. Finish easily as for Nectar.

Virgo 200 feet Very severe (hard)

Quite a serious little climb, with some interesting moves, up the right-angled corner left of Nectar. Start at the foot of the corner.

1 80 feet (5a). Climb the corner and pull awkwardly round the overhang at 35 feet into the groove on the right. Ascend this until a traverse right to the rib is necessary. Continue up easier rock to a ledge and block belay.
2 120 feet. Finish easily, as for Nectar.

The Gizzard 170 feet Very severe

A rather gloomy and unattractive-looking climb, often wet and greasy; the climbing, however, is not without interest and the positions are excellent. Start at a pile of blocks below a steep fist-wide crack in the left bounding wall of Virgo.

1 40 feet (4c). Step off the shattered blocks and climb the crack into a narrow sentry box; continue to a stance and belay.
2 70 feet (4c). Ascend the crack to below the ceiling. Traverse horizontally left to a steep corner, which leads to a large ledge.
3 60 feet (4c). Move left along the ledge for 10 feet and climb the steep wall direct on small holds; easier rocks above lead to the top.

Adam's Apple   150 feet   Very severe (hard)
The crack just left of The Gizzard.
1 90 feet (5a). Climb the crack to a junction with The Gizzard
   at the left end of the overhang. Follow the corner to the
   stance.
2 60 feet (4c). Move left and climb direct to the top.

Efrafa   165 feet   Extremely severe (E2)
The central corner of the crag is a fine feature; unfortunately it is
possible to escape to easier ground on the right. Start below the
corner.
1 115 feet (5c). Climb the corner for 65 feet to a smooth section
   and traverse left for 10 feet into a shallow corner. Go up this
   over a bulge, then move back right to a ledge.
2 50 feet. Continue up the line of the corner to the top.

**Razor Crack   230 feet   Very severe (hard)
The superb crack splitting the wall left of Efrafa gives steep,
exciting climbing on good holds; protection is more than adequate.
1 110 feet (5a). Climb the crack over several overhangs to a large
   ledge.
2 120 feet. Follow cracks and slabs to the top.

**Gillette   115 feet   Extremely severe (E2)
A magnificent little climb, steep and with sustained technical
interest. Start as for Razor Crack.
1 115 feet (5c). Follow Razor Crack to the small overhang at
   15 feet and move left, with difficulty, onto a narrow slab.
   Climb this and the steeper continuation groove; fine and
   difficult all the way. Walk off to the left. (The original way
   avoided the steep upper section by the rib on the right.)

Cut-throat   115 feet   Extremely severe (E2)
Start to the left of Razor Crack.
1 115 feet (5c). Climb an overhanging crack to join Gillette.
   Move right onto the rib and climb an obvious crack to join
   the original finish to Gillette.

**Mithrandir   110 feet   Very severe (hard)
A direct ascent of Gandalf's Groove; fine sustained climbing with
good protection. Start below the obvious groove, left of Gillette.
1 110 feet (5a). Climb the groove direct to a steep finish.

*Gandalf's Groove 120 feet Extremely severe (E1)

A varied climb of character and interest. Start below the groove.

1 120 feet (5b). Follow the groove for about 55 feet, when a descending traverse can be made to the rib on the left. Climb the rib, with some difficulty, to an obvious traverse back into the corner and finish up this.

Aragorn 130 feet Extremely severe (E2)

A contrived line, but gives some interesting climbing. Start as for Gandalf's Groove.

1 130 feet (5c). Follow the groove to the first bulge, move left and traverse the undercut slab to a spike on the arête. Climb into the niche above; go up this and make some difficult moves left into a groove. Move up to join Cravat and follow it for a few feet. Continue up the groove to the obvious steep crack and finish up this with considerable difficulty.

Cravat 115 feet Very severe (mild)

Short and steep; difficulties are well maintained and the climb is a satisfying one. Start at the extreme left end of the crag in a grassy corner.

1 115 feet (4b). Ascend the grassy corner to a ledge beneath a steep wall. Climb a thin crack, at the right end of the ledge, to a line of holds which lead right, into a scoop. Follow the scoop to a ledge, step right and follow the obvious line which zigzags up the left wall of Gandalf's Groove.

Wilkinson's Sword 90 feet Extremely severe (E4)†

Start at the same point as Cravat.

1 90 feet (6b). Climb a thin crack and move left into a groove which leads to a ledge. Make a hard finish up the thin crack above.

The Girdle Traverse 200 feet Very severe

A rather unsatisfactory right to left traverse. Start at the foot of The Neckband.

1 85 feet. Climb the rib for 35 feet, make a short traverse left and ascend the pleasant arête of Nectar to a ledge.

2 60 feet (4b). Traverse left along the ledge, go up a little and make an awkward traverse left, round a nose to a block belay.

3 55 feet (4c). Continue left along the ledge for 15 feet to a thin crack (peg runner). Finish by either traversing below the overhang or, more delicately, across the wall above it. Walk off to the left.

Tattered Banners   280 feet   Extremely severe (E2)
A much more satisfactory girdle. Start as for Virgo.
1 110 feet (5a). Climb Virgo to the overhang at 25 feet and move
   straight into the corner on the left. Follow this for 20 feet and
   traverse horizontally, crossing The Gizzard, to gain the arête
   just below a small bulge, by some loose flakes. Peg belay.
   (This is 20 feet below the exit of The Gizzard at the left of the
   overhang.)
2 50 feet (5c). Move up left to a large block, then descend a little
   until it is possible to move leftwards across the smooth corner
   of Efrafa to reach a small corner. Gain the cracks on the left
   and go down on undercuts until a traverse leads below the
   overhang to a belay in Razor Crack.
3 50 feet (5a). Move left to the rib and descend 10 feet, when it is
   possible to move into Gandalf's Groove. Traverse left, as
   for that climb; belay midway across the traverse.
4 70 feet (5b). Continue the traverse and go up the rib of Gandalf's
   Groove. Step left and finish up the steep crack of Aragorn.

Bowfell Links (244065)

The links lie on the Eskdale side of Bowfell just above Three
Tarns. There are twelve short chimneys or gullies, mostly of
the chockstone variety, but the rock is poor, uninteresting and
liberally provided with scree.

MINOR CRAGS

Scout Crag (299069)

An easily accessible crag, suitable for any weather conditions, lying low down on the fell beyond the foot of White Ghyll, some 15 minutes walk from Stickle Barn. The climbs are described from right to left.

Ramblers' Hangover   140 feet   Very difficult

An entertaining climb. Start below a small overhang (usually wet) at the foot of the crag, about 50 feet right of the well-marked start of Route 1.

1 40 feet. Climb the overhang, or the easier chimney on its right, and continue up slabs to a broad ledge.

2 50 feet. Ascend the diamond-shaped wall to a ledge, pull over a bulge and traverse left to a recess at the foot of a scoop. (It is possible to climb straight up the arête above the bulge to easy ground at the top.)

3 50 feet. Go up the groove past the overhang, step left (excellent belays) and cross a gully. Climb obliquely left up a mossy wall to a junction with Route 1, which leads easily to the top.

Zero Route   115 feet   Very difficult

A pleasant little climb. Start about 10 feet right of the obvious well-marked start of Route 1, at a steep little wall streaked with black.

1 45 feet. Ascend the 20 foot wall, past a small ledge half-way and continue up the easy slabs above to a stance and belay.

2 70 feet. Go up a shallow groove left of the stance to a junction with Route 1.

*Route 1   150 feet   Difficult

A popular route, rather polished but on very good rock. Start at the foot of a short wall below a holly.

1 45 feet. Climb the wall to the holly, followed by a polished slab on the left; then step right and go up to a ledge just below and to the right of a small overhang.

2 105 feet. Traverse right and climb more or less direct to a ledge. Finish up easy slabs.

Route 1·5   135 feet   Very difficult
The face midway between Routes 1 and 2. The lower portion is dirty and unpleasant in wet conditions.

1 40 feet. Climb easily up to a mossy crack in a shallow V-groove and ascend it for about 12 feet. Make a move to the right and ascend to a stance.

2 35 feet. Ascend the wall, turning the overhang on the left.

3 60 feet. Finish easily up the slabs.

Route 2   165 feet   Difficult
Start from a 2 foot high cave at the foot of a detached spur of rock, left of, and slightly lower down than Route 1.

1 20 feet. Go up the rightward slanting scoop to a terrace.

2 45 feet. Turn the short undercut crack on the left and climb round to the right to a ledge and oak belay (the crack is Severe).

3 40 feet. Traverse 10 feet right; then go up the steep wall on good holds to a belay in the groove on the right.

4 60 feet. Step back left and climb easy-angled slabs to the finish.

Variation
A little easier than the parent climb.

3a 100 feet. Traverse left for a few feet to a nose; then go straight up, finishing up a prominent black-streaked slab. Stances are available from time to time.

Scout's Belt   285 feet   Very difficult
A right to left traverse; though rather contrived and covered in vegetation in places, it provides quite pleasant climbing. Start at the foot of Zero Route.

1 45 feet. Ascend the 20 foot wall, past a small ledge half way, and continue up the easy slabs above to a stance and belay.

2 70 feet. Climb the wall on the left of the shallow groove of Zero Route, working leftwards after a few feet, and finishing by the arête on Route 1.

3 25 feet. Make a descending traverse to the belay in the groove on Route 2.

4 55 feet. The next belay is the tree visible round the arête on the left. It is reached by traversing narrow ledges to cross a heathery groove on to the arête; descend this to the tree. groove on to the arête; descend this to the tree.

5 50 feet. Cross the juniper ledge into a corner level with the top of an obvious horizontal crack. Make a short descent down steep vegetated rock below the corner; then traverse left past bulging rocks, using the horizontal crack, to a large spike belay.

6 40 feet. Traverse easily left to the scree gully.

About 50 yards to the right of the main crag, at a higher level, is a shorter, steeper and more heavily vegetated buttress. It has one clean worthwhile route.

Salmon Leap 110 feet Very severe
Start below the big overhanging nose at the right end of the crag. The climb takes a corner on the left of the nose, and is usually wet.
1 40 feet (4a). Climb steeply, on good holds to a belay just below and right of the nose.
2 70 feet (4c). Traverse left under the nose and enter the groove on its left side. Climb the left wall to the overhangs and pull over these to easy ground and the top.

Lower Scout Crag

Situated a few hundred feet directly below the main crag, Lower Scout Crag offers two short, but steep climbs with a number of variations. The better of the two climbs, **The Slab** (Severe), starts from the right-angled corner in the centre of the crag and runs up the right-bounding wall (the small pinnacle rocks alarmingly and should be treated carefully). A few feet to the left of The Slab, a cracked wall gives a steep climb on magnificent holds at about Severe standard.

By combining routes on the lower crags with climbs in White Ghyll and on Pavey Ark an enjoyable if circuitous approach to the Pikes can be made, comparable with the one via Middlefell Buttress and Gimmer.

Tarn Crag (290075)

Of similar interest to Scout Crag, Tarn Crag is suitable for training purposes or as an aperitif to the more serious fare on Pavey Ark. Situated on the immediate right of Mill Ghyll, about 200 feet below the level of Stickle Tarn, it is best reached by following the path up the true left side of the Ghyll, until a track leads off right to the foot of the crag.

A broad buttress, on which the first four routes lie, is separated from the well-defined ridge, containing Route 1 and Rib and Wall, by a grassy amphitheatre. A tongue of rock, covered with vegetation and topped by a conspicuous oak, runs up the middle of the amphitheatre to join the steeper rocks above; here lies Blandish. None of the routes are continuously steep and the sense of exposure is usually slight. The routes are described from left to right.

West Buttress   130 feet   Difficult
Start at the foot of the first steep wall, marked by a holly high on the left.
1 50 feet. Climb the wall, passing just to the right of the holly, and go up a short groove to a ledge.
2 80 feet. Traverse left for 10 feet to a rib which leads, after 30 feet to easy rocks.

Route 2   130 feet   Difficult
Start at the lowest point of the buttress, 15 feet to the right of West Buttress.
1 70 feet. Go up steep rocks to a narrow ledge, step left and climb straight up on good holds to a ledge and belay.
2 60 feet. Finish up broken rocks.

Heather Slab   135 feet   Very Difficult
A smooth triangular slab, which lies just inside the right-hand rib of the buttress. Start just left of centre.
1 30 feet. Climb the slab and exit left to a recess.
2 45 feet. Traverse 15 feet left and climb a steep but easy corner to a sloping ledge.
3 60 feet. Follow the groove on the right to an easy arête which leads to easy ground and the summit.

Orchid   285 feet   Severe (mild)
Start a few feet right of Heather Slab below a steep crack.
1 50 feet. Climb the crack to a ledge.
2 70 feet. Follow the shallow chimney, past a small pinnacle, and move out leftwards. Go up to another ledge.
3 50 feet. Traverse easily rightwards, passing a rowan and continue to the left end of a ledge. From here make a short ascent to the foot of a groove.
4 35 feet. Climb the groove, awkward at the top, then step right and continue to a ledge below a slab.
5 80 feet. Go up the left edge of the slab and finish up broken rocks.

Blandish   180 feet   Very difficult
Start by scrambling up to a prominent oak situated high up the tongue of rock covered with vegetation, which runs up the middle of the amphitheatre.
1 20 feet. Climb the wall behind the tree to a ledge.
2 70 feet. Continue up the steep rib above, using a thin crack on its left, until a traverse right leads to a corner.
3 90 feet. Go up a short wall, then a steep groove to easier rocks leading to the top.

Rib and Wall   130 feet   Difficult

Start 10 feet left of the right-bounding ridge of the grassy amphitheatre, at a subsidiary rib.

1 55 feet. Go straight up the middle of the rib to a ledge.
2 75 feet. Continue up the wall above to a small ledge; then
   traverse left to an awkward finish up a steep groove.

Route 1   110 feet   Difficult

The well-marked route up the right-bounding ridge of the grassy
amphitheatre. Start just to the left of the foot of the ridge.

1 50 feet. Go up a few feet and traverse right to the nose, where
   easy climbing leads to a good stance.
2 60 feet. Finish up broken rocks.

Harrison Stickle (282073)

The summit crags of Harrison Stickle, impressive as they are
when seen from a distance, prove disappointingly broken on
close inspection. Several routes have been recorded on the west
face but none seems to merit detailed description; innumerable
variations are possible.

Harristickorner (85 feet, Very difficult) takes the well-scratched
corner where the north and west faces meet. **Porphyry Slab**
(240 feet, Very difficult) follows a broad mossy slab, starting in a
grassy bay about 70 yards right of Harristickorner.

Pike o' Stickle (273073)

A large sweep of rock, just below the summit and facing Bowfell,
is impressive to look at but disappointing to climb. Basically, the
crag is sound, but carries an unusually large quantity of perched
blocks. Lines are conspicuous by their absence and it is possible
to climb anywhere at about Very difficult/mild Severe standard. A
little buttress on the right side of the gully, on the immediate
right of the Pike gives **Merlin Slab** (280 feet Difficult). The
climb starts from a slab leading into a huge white scoop, opposite
the man-made cave, and finishes up a blunt rib above.

Side Pike (293054)

This lies on the extreme right of Lingmoor Fell, as seen from the
Old Dungeon Ghyll Hotel. The approach is from the cattle grid
at the top of the Blea Tarn road. A path runs straight up the
hillside and over the top of the crag. The climbs are described
from right to left.

Tinning's Move   110 feet   Severe (mild)
Start just left of the wire fence and 10 feet right of the obvious crack.
1 70 feet. Climb the wall to a ledge, pull over the bulge on the left and go slightly right into a shallow corner, which leads to a good ledge.
2 40 feet. Finish directly up cleaned rock.

Spider Crack   110 feet   Severe (mild)
The prominent crack, overhanging near the bottom; quite awkward when wet. Start a few yards left of the wire fence.
1 25 feet. Avoid the overhang by climbing the steep wall on the left for about 15 feet followed by an awkward traverse right into the crack.
2 35 feet. Climb the crack to a large ledge.
3 50 feet. Finish up the mossy rocks on the left.

To the left of Spider Crack is a short stretch of steep wall, seamed with thin cracks; this has been climbed in two or three places, but the routes do not warrant description.

Limpet Grooves   80 feet   Very severe (mild)
The deep overhanging groove left of the mossy wall gives a short climb of character and interest. Start at the foot of the groove by a large detached pinnacle.
1 80 feet (4b). Ascend the right wall of the groove for about 10 feet, make a long stride into the groove, move up a little and traverse back across the right wall to a small ledge. Finish up the overhanging groove above.

A ledge on the left may be reached by walking behind the pinnacle; two routes of rather less interest start here. **Rough Ridge** (110 feet, Very difficult) follows a narrow slab slanting up to a holly tree and then a groove, finishing up the right hand rib of the groove. **Marrawak** (110 feet, Severe) ascends the wall directly below the tree, then continues rightwards onto the front of the buttress, where a short crack leads to a tree and easier ground.
A girdle of the crag has been worked out, starting at Limpet Grooves and finishing up Spider Crack; the line is obvious and the standard, Very severe.

Raven Crag Walthwaite (325058)

This is the conspicuous outcrop on the hillside immediately north-east of Chapel Stile, easily reached from the Red Bank road. It offers climbing suitable for a wet day and one or two better climbs useful for a short afternoon or evening. The climbs are described from left to right.

Route 1 (Severe), is the well marked wall above the large holly at the extreme left end of the crag. Round the rib on the right is a wide recess bounded on its right side by the wide overhanging **Walthwaite Crack** (Very severe). The wall of the recess is taken by **Hardup Wall** (Severe) and **Walthwaite Chimney** (Severe) follows the long tree-filled groove on the other side of the rib to the right.

Alfresco 110 feet Severe (hard)
Start mid-way between Walthwaite Chimney and the small ash that marks the start of Route 2.
1 110 feet. Go up the first little wall onto a glacis; continue directly up and then trend right to a small dead tree. Climb the bulge above with care to a good ledge and junction with Route 2. Finish up the short open groove.

Route 2 140 feet Severe
Steep and interesting, the best climb of its standard on the crag. Start at a small ash at the lowest point of the crag.
1 140 feet. Go up over a small nose to an oak at 60 feet. Move 10 feet left, climb a short scoop and traverse right for 10 feet. Climb back left to an overhanging rib, where a chimney leads right to the top.

Deuterus 120 feet Very severe
A large block has recently come off the initial part of the second pitch; in fact, this whole section requires care. Start a few feet to the right of Route 2.
1 30 feet. Ascend the wall direct to a good ledge.
2 90 feet (4c). Climb the overhanging scoop on the right, move left and go up to a recess on Route 2. Traverse right, round the rib and across the wall to another recess. Move right and climb directly to the top.

Protus   90 feet   Very severe
Steep, exposed and of considerable technical interest. Start at a holly about 30 feet right of Deuterus. There is an oak on the left and an elm above on the right.
1 30 feet (4b). Climb over an awkward bulge to the elm.
2 60 feet (5a). Descend a few feet and traverse delicately left; then go up a few feet, crossing a rib into a groove. Step left and pull out of the groove onto the exposed wall on the left. Ascend the wall to a recess (junction with Deuterus), move right and climb directly to the top.

Walthwaite Gully   90 feet   Very severe (mild)
The corner between the main crag and the slabby right wing. Short and dank, but worthy for all that. Start at the foot of the corner.
1 30 feet (4b). Climb the corner crack to the right end of the belay ledge on Protus.
2 60 feet (4c). Climb the flake crack on the right, up to, and through the huge yew tree to the top.

Girdle Traverse   310 feet   Very severe
A left to right girdle starting at Route 1.
Go up Route 1 for about 50 feet; then step right, round the corner and cross the top of Hardup Wall to belay above the crack of Walthwaite Crack. Climb over blocks and descend the tree-filled groove of Walthwaite Chimney until it is possible to make a delicate step on to the right-hand rib. Traverse across to a stance on Alfresco. Go along the 10 foot traverse of Route 2 and continue across the traverse of Deuterus to Protus. Finish up Protus.

Oak Howe Crag (305055)

The crag lies fairly high on the south-west ridge of Lingmoor, half an hour from Stickle Barn. It is best approached from there by crossing the bridge almost opposite, passing through the farmyard, then turning left and keeping fairly low until the ridge itself is reached. The abrupt ascent of this is simpler than crossing through the dense juniper higher up the fellside. The main interest provided by the crag is Oak Howe Needle, a detached pinnacle, which gives a number of short climbs.

Spout Crag

This is the crag about 300 yards south of Oak Howe Needle. The descent from the top of the crag is well to the right.

Crossword 190 feet Very severe

A serious climb, which starts about the centre of the steep lower face, just to the right of a holly.

1 50 feet. Pull over an overhang into a niche and climb a crack to a ledge on the right. Traverse right to a recess.

2 45 feet. Climb the overhanging wall on the left to a recess and traverse right to a birch.

3 70 feet. Ascend the easier wall on the left, moving right to an oak.

4 25 feet. Climb the steep wall behind the oak to finish.

Gurt Gardin Stuff 220 feet Very severe

Start 25 feet to the right of Crossword, at a leftward-facing corner.

1 100 feet. Move up into a groove and climb the rib on its right to ledges. Pull up the steep wall to the flake on the left and go up the steep groove above. Cross pitch 2 of Crossword and continue up to some trees. Go left to a birch below a brown wall.

2 120 feet. Move up and to the right to a mossy corner. Climb this, then traverse left on an obvious line. Move up to a higher line, traverse right and pull out to easier rock. Go steeply up left, then continue rightwards to the top to a tree belay well back.

Upper Spout Crag

This is the crag which lies south-east of Oak Howe Crags directly above the quarry. The easiest approach starts from the campsite at Chapel Stile. Walk up to Baysbrown Farm and continue up the quarry track. Go round the back of the quarry to the crag. The main buttress is split by two obvious crack lines giving good routes.

Dinsdale 120 feet Extremely severe (E2)

The obvious left hand crack. Start below the crack.

1 120 feet (5b). Climb the crack, past a holly and an overhang at 80 feet.

Spiny Norman 150 feet Extremely severe (E3)

The right hand crack. Start just right of the toe of the buttress.

1 120 feet (6a). Climb up for 10 feet and traverse left to a 'V' groove. Climb this, then move left onto a slab; move back right into the groove (crux) which leads to an overhanging crack. Climb this, then move up and leftwards to a small holly. Go across right to a large holly and belay.

2 30 feet. Finish easily.

Kettle Crag (279050)

This is the lowest crag on the slopes of Pike o' Blisco, facing Wall End Farm. The left wall of a wide grassy gully at the right hand side gives some short climbs of Severe to Very severe standard.

Gladstone Knott (253046)

Situated 400 yards from the head of Crinkle Gill, on the left and facing east. It has five climbable chimneys of about Difficult standard. The rock is poor and vegetated and the crag cannot be recommended.

Crinkle Crag (250050)

Opposite Gladstone Knott, on the right side of Crinkle Gill and just below the summit of the highest Crinkle, is a large broken looking crag. **Terrace Crack** (170 feet, Severe) follows a line of cracks just right of the impressive 80-foot central pillar. The pinnacle belay of pitch 2 is an obvious landmark.

Blake Rigg (285040)

This slow-drying crag, which lies on the shoulder of Pike o' Blisco, overlooking Blea Tarn, consists of steep walls broken by grassy terraces. A number of climbs have been recorded but, although there are some good pitches, they do not warrant description.

EASEDALE

The usual approach to these crags is from Grasmere. There is a municipal car-park on the edge of the village, adjacent to the road leading to Easedale; parking is not permitted further up the valley. Blea Crag and Deer Bield Crag can also be reached from Great Langdale.

Helm Crag (328093)

The obvious little crag 100 yards behind the quarry at the start of the Helm Crag track from Easedale. The central buttress is steep and clean and, within its limits, offers suitable climbing for a short day. The climbs are described from left to right.

Beacon Rib   85 feet   Very severe (hard)
The blunt arête on the left of the crag. Start at the foot of the arête.
1 55 feet (5a). Climb just to the left of the rib for a few feet before gaining the crest, which leads to a ledge and block belay.
2 30 feet (5a). Go up the scoop to a fine platform, move right into Beacon Crack and finish up this.

Beacon Crack   80 feet   Severe (hard)
The prominent, wide corner-crack gives a strenuous climb.
1 80 feet. Climb the crack.

Holly-tree Crack   120 feet   Very difficult
The obvious steep crack facing Beacon Crack, and a few yards to the right. The second pitch can be split if necessary.
1 40 feet. Climb the steep crack, which is the hardest part of the climb, to a ledge.
2 80 feet. Move a few feet to the right and go straight up over doubtful blocks to a holly. Climb through this and continue to the plantation above. Move right along a ledge and finish up a short wall.

Flarepath   100 feet   Very severe
Delicate and quite sustained. The route crosses Holly-tree Crack
and finishes at the top of Beacon Crack. Start at a steep corner
right of Holly-tree Crack.
1 40 feet (4c). Climb the crack in the corner to the top of pitch
   1, Holly-tree Crack.
2 60 feet (4c). Follow the open groove on the left for a few feet
   until a move can be made left onto a slab. Traverse delicately
   upwards to a ledge with a large detached block and then step
   across for the last few feet of Beacon Crack.

Flarepath Direct   90 feet   Very severe (hard)
The chimney-groove line directly above pitch 1 of Holly-tree
Crack. Steep, direct and easily the hardest route on the crag.
Start a few feet right of Flarepath.
1 40 feet (4c). Climb the corner crack to the belay ledge.
2 50 feet (5a). Climb the first few moves of Flarepath; then step
   boldly round the rib on the right into a steep shallow groove.
   Go up this and make a difficult and strenuous entry into the
   chimney above, which then leads more easily to the top.

The Grouter   105 feet   Severe
Start in a wooded corner 30 yards right of Beacon Crack.
1 60 feet. Climb a short crack and grassy groove into a recess.
   Pull out left; then move up to the overhang and step left to
   a good stance.
2 30 feet. Traverse to the right, below the overhang, to a very
   steep corner which leads to a crevasse. There is a large stance
   just above.
3 15 feet. Climb the crack behind a pinnacle on the right.

Bentley   115 feet   Very difficult
A surprisingly good route up the overgrown right wing of the
crag. Start in the wooded corner, as for The Grouter.
1 65 feet. Climb a rightward-slanting flake-crack in a slab to a
   grove of trees and continue up a fist-wide crack in the corner
   to a ledge with a tree, below a steep arête. Step left along the
   ledge, round the arête, where a short steep crack leads up into
   an impressive corner. (A Very severe alternative to the short
   crack is a gangway slanting left behind the tree.)
2 50 feet. Follow the corner over a bulge at the top onto a short
   slab and up to the finishing terrace.

Rainbow (250 feet, Very severe (hard)) girdles the crag from the
tree, left of Beacon Rib, to finish up Bentley. The line is fairly
obvious and as such, does not require description.

Gibson Knott (317100)

This steep, vegetation-covered crag lies on the north slopes of Far Easedale, a little above the stepping stones and some 400 feet above the valley. **Route 1** (Difficult) takes a line up the right side of the crag, but only has about 40 feet of real climbing. **Route 2** (235 feet, Difficult) follows a line just left of a steep chimney near the left end of the crag and is rather more continuous.

Blea Crag (301080)

This crag lies above Easedale Tarn on the south-side of the route to Pavey Ark and is about twenty minutes walk from the tarn. It is steep and somewhat broken and is split by a wide fan of vegetation. A notable feature is the big vegetated ledge cutting the left half of the crag at about 70 feet.

Sorbo   215 feet   Very severe (hard)
The first pitch follows a slabby groove to the left end of the vegetated ledge. The second pitch takes a fine long groove up the middle of the wall above.
1 75 feet (5a). Go up a series of three grassy ledges to a juniper and the foot of a slabby groove. Climb the left wall of the groove before trending back slightly right to gain the left end of the vegetated ledge. Go right for 25 feet to the foot of the groove.
2 90 feet (4c). Climb to the second of two grass ledges; then follow the bed of the corner to a large ledge.
3 50 feet. Follow the clean rib on the left to the top.

Blea Rigg Climb   185 feet   Very difficult
Quite a serious route for the grade. Start below the overhangs at the right end of the vegetated ledge.
1 95 feet. Scramble easily up a grassy rake and climb a square little scoop to an awkward exit onto the ledge.
2 90 feet. Traverse the steep wall on the right to the arête; climb up on small holds and follow the obvious line of weakness to the top.

Bleaberry Buttress   230 feet   Very severe (hard)

About 50 yards right of the vegetation fan, and starting from a small subsidiary terrace, is a narrow buttress of smooth rock. An interesting climb but with a lot of vegetation. Start up a prominent groove containing a pillar of three blocks.

1 95 feet (5a). Climb the groove and traverse right over a block on the rib and pull up into a niche. Move up and right, and follow two short scoops to a ledge at the foot of a couple of little rough slabs; climb these to a bilberry terrace.

2 55 feet (5a). Traverse the slab, inset in the impending wall, to the rib on the left; move round this onto steep rock and climb directly up to a grass ledge. A serious pitch.

3 80 feet (4c). Go up the scoops directly ahead and finish up the arête on the left.

DEER BIELD CRAG (303087)

Deer Bield Crag is a small, but impressively steep, crag situated on the true right side of Far Easedale, some three hundred feet above the path and about an hour's easy walk from Grasmere. It may be reached from Great Langdale in a rather longer time by way of Mill Ghyll and Stickle and Codale Tarns. The most prominent feature of the crag is its central buttress (actually completely detached), which houses two of the great climbs of the district, the classic Deer Bield Buttress and the modern, impressive Take it to the Limit. Two more outstanding climbs make use of the fissure between this buttress and the parent crag: Deer Bield Crack on the left and Deer Bield Chimney on the right.

To the left of the buttress is the recessed corner of Dunmail Cracks and the smooth wall of The Pendulum. To the right the cliff changes character with some deep slabby grooves and, notably, two prominent arêtes: Imagination and Pearls Before Swine.

The Pendulum 115 feet   Extremely severe (E2)
The main pitch is steep and somewhat intimidating. Start in a broken corner at the left end of a smooth and impressively steep wall.
1 30 feet. Climb the corner for 20 feet and step onto a small rock ledge on the right, level with an obvious traverse line across the wall.
2 45 feet (5b). Step right and make a couple of hard moves onto the gangway. Continue rightwards along this to a short overhanging groove and climb this strenuously to a grassy stance on the right.
3 40 feet (4c). Move round the arête and up to a flake. Step left and continue to the top.

Stiletto 120 feet   Extremely severe (E3)
The thin crack leading up to the right end of the traverse of Pendulum. Start 25 feet right of Pendulum, at a steep groove just left of a tree.
1 120 feet (6a). Climb the groove to a ledge on the right, then continue up the flake on the left and the crack above to the Pendulum traverse. Follow the crack through the overhang and go up to a sloping ledge on the right, where a thin crack leads up an overhanging wall to a niche; finish more easily.

*The Graduate   150 feet   Extremely severe (E3)

The slim groove on the right hand edge of the smooth wall gives a good steep climb. Start at an obvious flake, 10 feet left of Dunmail Cracks.

1 50 feet (5b). Climb the overhanging groove parallel to Dunmail Cracks and exit left at its top onto a ledge. Follow the crack to easier ground and belay well back in the recess.

2 100 feet (6a). Traverse left to a block on the arête and pull up to gain the base of a steep groove. Climb the groove, peg runner, to a ledge at its top. Surmount a bulge on good holds and follow the arête, joining the last few feet of Pendulum.

Dunmail Cracks   100 feet   Very severe (hard)

The left corner of the amphitheatre containing the two companion cracks of Deer Bield, the other being the classic Deer Bield Crack. A serious and not particularly attractive climb; the major difficulty lies in the first pitch, but nowhere is it easy. Start at an embedded pinnacle below the centre of the amphitheatre.

1 55 feet (5a). Go up a short steep wall to the foot of a broken-looking groove; climb this until an overhang bars the way. Break out left onto the wall and get into a short crack with some difficulty. Go up to a good ledge and continue over some large flakes to another ledge.

2 35 feet (4c). Climb the crack at the left end of the ledge to a small ledge and follow the crack in the corner to a stance. The left side of the crack is formed by a large detached block and should be treated with care.

3 80 feet (5a). Climb up the outside edge of the crack and continue up the corner to the top.

Gymslip   185 feet   Extremely severe (E3)

A serious and technically demanding climb up the unattractive looking wall between the two cracks; much better than appearances suggest. Start as for Deer Bield Crack.

1 80 feet (4b). Pitch 1 Deer Bield Crack.

2 80 feet (5c). Swing up left onto the base of the innocent-looking ramp. Climb this with difficulty and the shallow groove above, when a short crack on the left leads to a ledge. Swing right round the rib to the ledge below the Amen Corner of Deer Bield Crack.

3 25 feet (5b). Climb the obvious slanting groove on the left to the top.

**Deer Bield Crack 170 feet Very severe (hard)

A climb of great character and interest, requiring considerable energy and perseverance. The famous chimney pitch is probably unique of its type, and the final overhang is sufficiently problematical to leave the outcome in doubt until the very end. It may often be found dry after, or even during a period of rain. Start at an upstanding flake slightly to the left of the lowest point of the buttress.

1 80 feet (4b). Go up the crack above the flake for about 6 feet and make a long stride to a small niche on the right. Follow the slab on the left for 10 feet to reach the line of the crack and climb it to the foot of the obvious deep chimney.

2 35 feet (4c). The crux. Climb the chimney deeply inside as long as possible; eventually it is necessary to traverse out under the overhang and a short and very strenuous ascent leads to a small ledge on the left.

3 55 feet (4c). Continue up the now narrow crack to a recess below a "super Amen Corner". Go up the overhanging crack on the right to finish on splendid holds.

***Deer Bield Buttress 185 feet Extremely severe (E1)

An exceedingly fine climb, combining considerable technical interest and difficulty with fine positions. In its lower half the climb is strenuous, and in the upper, delicate. Strenuous or otherwise it is never easy. Start about 10 feet right of Deer Bield Crack.

1 60 feet (5a). Climb the scoop and move left under the overhang to join Deer Bield Crack. Go up this to the foot of a sharply overhanging crack just on the right. Climb the crack (strenuous) to a belay on the edge overlooking Deer Bield Crack.

2 35 feet (5a). The first crux. Traverse across the slab on the right to an overhanging groove and gain a tiny ledge on its left-hand rib. Continue past a ledge and a short steep section to a small stance.

3 90 feet (5b). Climb "the long groove", taking the right-hand branch when it divides, to where it peters out; climb up for a few feet and traverse delicately right into a scoop. Go up left to the top of the pinnacle, which gives a good belay but no stance, below and to the right of the second crux. Swing left to a sharp-edged flake and continue traversing, delicately, to a thin crack, which is climbed to the top. It is also possible to finish direct from the sharp-edged flake; shorter and sharper.

Variation   **El Dorado**   120 feet   Extremely severe (E2)
Start from the stance below "the long groove" of Deer Bield
Buttress.
4a 120 feet (5b). Traverse down and left to a groove in the nose.
   Climb the groove and pull out right at the top. Move across
   a slab to a shallow groove (junction with Peccadillo). Go up
   and back left to the rib and follow this to the top (as for
   Peccadillo).

**Peccadillo   180 feet   Extremely severe (E4)
The steep bottomless groove, set in the rib right of Deer Bield
Buttress is the main feature of this steep and precarious climb.
Start as for Deer Bield Buttress.
1 100 feet (6a). Climb straight up the scoop and step round right
   onto a narrow slab on the face. Climb up and traverse delicately
   left to the base of the bottomless groove. Climb this (peg runner)
   to a good spike on the right arête. Move left across the slab
   to join Deer Bield Buttress. Go up this for 20 feet to belay at
   the foot of "the long groove".
2 80 feet (5b). Climb the wall out on the left for 25 feet, then go
   up a shallow groove until moves left can be made onto the
   arête. Follow this to the top.

*Desperado   190 feet   Extremely severe (E5)
An interesting route up the face right of Deer Bield Buttress. The
line is intricate but unfortunately lacks independence. Start at
the foot of Deer Bield Chimney.
1 95 feet (6a). Climb the wall diagonally left to gain a ledge on
   Peccadillo. Step left and climb the groove of Peccadillo (peg
   runner) to a good spike on the right arête. Pull right onto the
   wall and move up to gain a sloping ledge below an overlap.
   Follow the break right for a few feet, then trend left up the wall
   to a ledge (top of pitch 2 Deer Bield Buttress).
2 65 feet (5c). Traverse right to the foot of an obvious groove.
   Climb this for 10 feet to a good flake hold. Swing out right
   onto the face and climb this, first trending right, then direct
   to the top of the huge pinnacle.
3 30 feet (4c). Step down and right into a cave. Climb a crack
   through the roof to finish.

*Take it to the Limit 190 feet Extremely severe (E5)
The smooth-looking face to the right of Desperado gives an exceedingly difficult climb in a most impressive and serious situation. Start at the foot of Deer Bield Chimney.
1 100 feet (6b). Climb the wall diagonally left to a ledge (as for Desperado). Step right from the right end of the ledge and pull up into a sickle-shaped depression (poor peg runner). Move up to the top of this; then go up right to reach a large block which protrudes from the Chimney. From the block traverse left to a hold in the middle of the wall. Move up and leftwards to reach a thin crack which slants rightwards across the wall. Follow this to better holds below the roof.
2 60 feet (5a). Follow a crack up to the right below the roof and pull through at a groove. Continue direct to a large spike belay (junction with Deer Bield Buttress).
3 30 feet (5a). Move right and climb the left hand-crack out of the cave to finish.

Deer Bield Chimney 175 feet Severe (hard)
Although an outstanding climb of its type, several recent rock-falls have made the climb dangerous and it is probably best left alone. Start by scrambling up to the foot of the obvious chimney.
1 45 feet. Climb the chimney, with an excursion out to the right at 15 feet.
2 40 feet. Climb up to the jammed boulders and find a way through them to reach a large and comfortable recess with a view into Deer Bield Crack.
3 40 feet. Climb out on the right and avoid the delicately poised blocks by making some awkward moves, just to their right. Belay above in a comfortable sentry box.
4 50 feet. Ascend the chimney and the smooth crack above to a large sloping ledge. Either walk off here or make a strenuous hand-traverse up to the right to finish.

Imagination 195 feet Extremely severe (E4)
The arête between Deer Bield Chimney and Hubris; it has a particularly bold and serious second pitch. Start below the arête.
1 65 feet (5a). Climb the stepped arête, mainly on the right-hand side, to a glacis below a steep wall. Step left and belay in the chimney.
2 130 feet (6a). Traverse to the right side of the glacis and climb the right wall of the arête to a good finger hold on the left. Pull up to a good hold, then make a long reach to more holds, where it is possible to reach the arête. Follow this to a bulge, pull over and continue more easily to the final steep rib which leads on small holds to the top.

*Hubris   175 feet   Extremely severe (E1)
The deep groove right of Imagination is considerably steeper and more difficult than its appearance suggests. Start by scrambling up easy slabs to the short corner which guards access to the groove.
1 55 feet (5a). Ascend the awkward corner and follow the groove to where a subsidiary groove leaves it on the left.
2 120 feet (5a). Climb the main groove for 10 feet and then move into the crack on the left. Climb this, with difficulty where it steepens, into the upper part of the groove. Finish up the groove.

Variation   An easier finish
2a 130 feet (5a). Follow the normal pitch to below the final groove, when a delicate move right leads to another groove on the right. Climb this to a tree belay. Grassy scrambling leads to the top.

**Pearls Before Swine   180 feet   Extremely severe (E3)
A fine route up the stepped arête between Hubris and Easedale Groove. Start by scrambling up easy slabs to the foot of Hubris.
1 150 feet (5c). Pull up onto the smooth slab on the right and climb it to the foot of a short steep corner which leads onto the crest of the arête. Climb the corner, (or the arête on the left) stepping right at the top and continue to a foothold below the first overlap. Move round to the left and make some difficult moves until it is possible to move back onto the crest at a good foothold. Move a little left and climb straight up to a large doubtful block. Pull over this and continue to a ledge and tree belay.
2 30 feet. Climb easily to the top.

Easedale Groove   170 feet   Severe
The slim groove right of Hubris gives a pleasant climb. Start by scrambling up easy slabs to the foot of Hubris.
1 80 feet. Go right along an easy traverse to the rib below and right of the groove. Climb the rib on sloping holds for a few feet; then go up to the first overhang that bars access to the groove proper. Pull round the overhang and follow the groove past another overhang to a stance.
2 40 feet. Climb up to the roof, make a couple of delicate steps to the right and go up to a tree belay.
3 30 feet. Finish easily up rock ribs and grass.

Eden Groove   210 feet   Severe (hard)
The very deep groove over the 'top' on the right of Easedale Groove, the least worthy route on the crag. Start in a grassy bay below an impending wall at the foot of the buttress.

1 50 feet. Step off from a small pedestal and climb the leftward-slanting corner-crack, which leads, with one or two awkward moves, into the easy-looking groove above. Follow this to its top.
2 40 feet (4b). Climb a little slab on the left below the impending wall and pull into the deep groove, which leads to another stance below a wide crack in the right wall.
3 70 feet (4b). Climb the left branch of the groove on its left side and climb a delicate little slab in the corner under the impending wall. Traverse left and climb up to a tree in the groove above. Scrambling remains.

A climb has been made to the right of Eden Groove, starting at the top of the first pitch; this is **Monkey Puzzle** (Severe). The tree, which gave the climb its name and much of its character, has now disappeared and it seems rather pointless.

The Girdle Traverse   340 feet   Extremely severe (E2)
Some good pitches linked by rather undistinguished climbing. Start as for Pendulum at the foot of a broken corner on the edge of the smooth wall at the left end of the crag.

1 75 feet (5b). Follow the corner for 20 feet and move out to a ledge up on the right. Traverse right with considerable difficulty along the obvious gangway to a niche. Pull out of this, awkwardly, and go up to a grassy stance on the right.
2 75 feet (4c). Step round the corner on the right and, on doubtful rock, traverse into Dunmail Cracks. Descend the crack to the large ledges at the foot of the chimney pitch on Deer Bield Crack.
3 20 feet. Cross Deer Bield Crack and go down to a ledge on the far side.
4 35 feet (5a). Move right across the easy-angled slab to an overhanging groove; gain a tiny ledge on its left hand rib and continue straight up to another small ledge. Go up over the bulge to a small stance. (This is the first crux of Deer Bield Buttress.)
5 55 feet (5b). Climb the groove above, taking the right hand branch, where it divides, and follow it until it peters out in a short wall a few feet below the obvious pinnacle. Move right into a scoop and go up left to the top of the pinnacle.
6 45 feet (5a). Descend the groove for a few feet and stride across the smooth slab on the right to an overhung ledge.

Make an exit from the right-hand end via an undercut, slanting V-chimney to gain the foot of the smooth crack of Deer Bield Chimney.

7 35 feet (4c). Climb the smooth crack and finish by a strenuous traverse rightwards.

The New Girdle 410 feet Extremely Severe (E3)†
A complete right to left girdle at about half-height. Start at the foot of Eden Groove.

1 140 feet (5a). Climb Eden Groove for 60 feet to the bottom of a long grassy groove. Move up the wall on the left, traverse round the arête beneath a bulge and step down into Easedale Groove. Go up leftwards to the arête of Pearls before Swine and traverse left to the stance on Hubris.

2 70 feet (5c). Climb the steep groove on the left to where the angle eases. Traverse left to the arête of Imagination and continue into Deer Bield Chimney. Descend, with care, for 20 feet to a large block belay.

3 30 feet (5b). Move left out of the chimney onto a slab. Traverse horizontally left to the foot of "the long groove" of Deer Bield Buttress.

4 30 feet (5b). Step down and move left to a slab on the arête. Traverse into Deer Bield Crack and move down to large ledges.

5 50 feet. Go left along the ledge, over a large block, to a belay on Stiletto.

6 90 feet (5c). Climb the crack of Stiletto for 60 feet to the sloping ledge below the final wall. Move left round the corner and continue along easy ledges to finish.

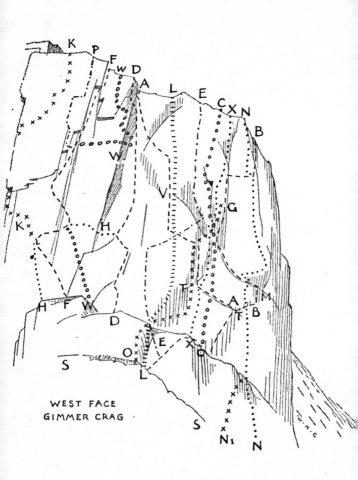

WEST FACE
GIMMER CRAG

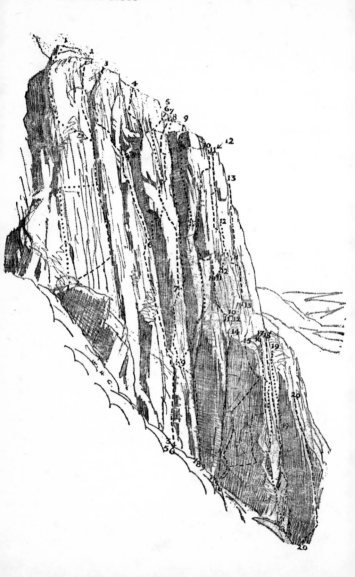

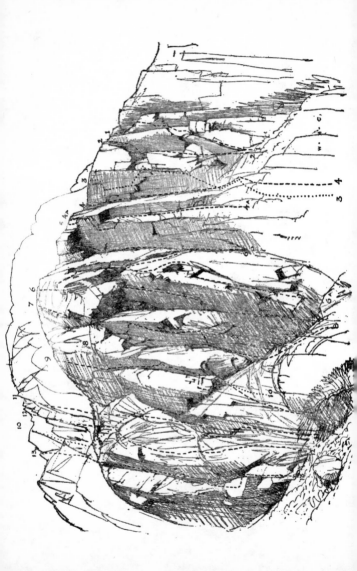

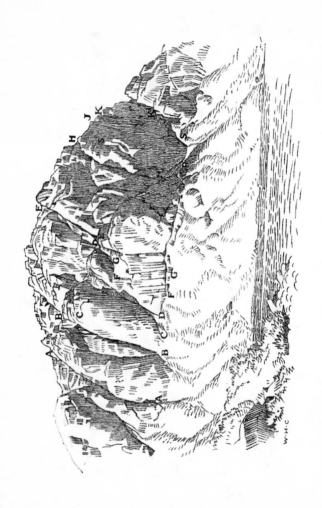

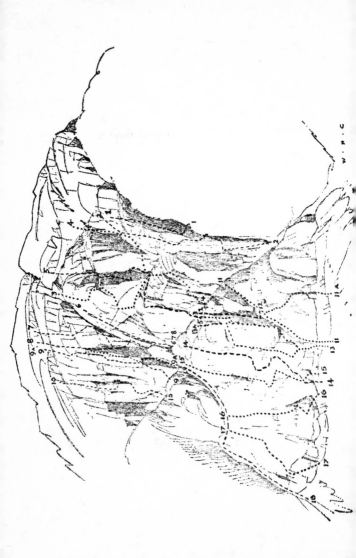

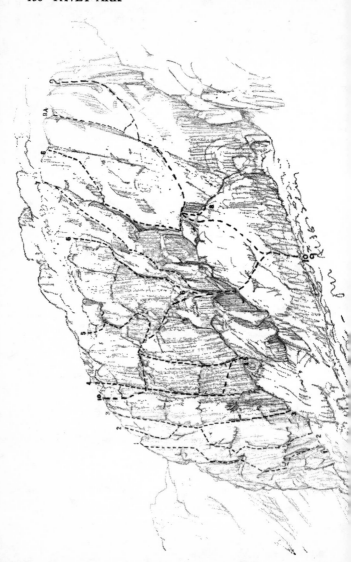

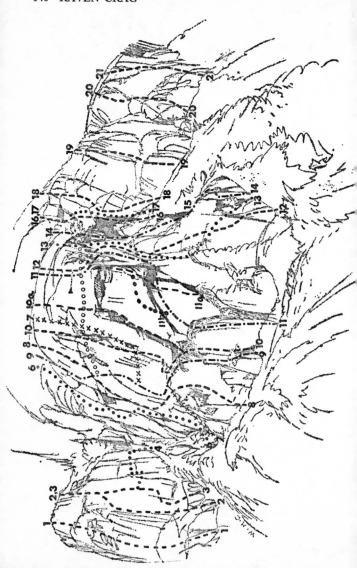

GRADED LIST OF CLIMBS

EXTREMELY SEVERE (continued)

*Cascade Direct	Pavey Ark	68
Cut-Throat	Neckband Crag	96
Dinsdale	Upper Spout Crag	107
Efrafa	Neckband Crag	96
Eliminot	White Ghyll	42
*Equus	Gimmer Crag	23
**Gillette	Neckband Crag	96
Girdle Traverse, The	Deer Bield Crag	119
*Haste Not Direct	White Ghyll	43
Hobbit, The	Pavey Ark	50
Karma	White Ghyll	41
Kudos	Pavey Ark	66
Mindbender	North Buttress, Bowfell	88
Pendulum, The	Deer Bield Crag	113
Ragmans Trumpet, The	Pavey Ark	50
Risus	Pavey Ark	65
Sally Free and Easy	Pavey Ark	51
Slip Knot Variations	White Ghyll	38
Solaris	Flat Crag, Bowfell	85
*Startrek	Pavey Ark	68
Tattered Banners	Neckband Crag	97
*White Ghyll Eliminate	White Ghyll	43

E1

Aardvark	Pavey Ark	58
Babylon	East Raven Crag	82
Bowfell Buttress Eliminate	Bowfell Buttress	92
*Chimney Variant	White Ghyll	44
***Deer Bield Buttress	Deer Bield Crag	115
Dight	Gimmer Crag	28
Do Not	White Ghyll	37
Fastburn	Flat Crag, Bowfell	86
Feet of Clay	White Ghyll	36
Flat Iron Wall	Flat Crag, Bowfell	86
*Gandalf's Groove	Neckband Crag	97
Gimmer High Girdle	Gimmer Crag	27
**Gimmer String	Gimmer Crag	26
*Hubris	Deer Bield Crag	118
Joker's Slab	East Raven Crag	80
*Man of Straw	White Ghyll	36
Poacher Right Hand	Gimmer Crag	23
Poker Face	Pavey Ark	57
Rainmaker, The	Pavey Ark	55
Red Groove	Pavey Ark	65
Rib, The	Pavey Ark	60
Rubicon Groove	Bowfell Buttress	91
Sinistral	Pavey Ark	50
Slowburn	Flat Crag, Bowfell	85
*Spring Bank	Gimmer Crag	21
*Sword of Damocles	North Buttress, Bowfell	88

EXTREMELY SEVERE (continued)

Variation Girdle Traverse	White Ghyll	47
Waste Not, Want Not	White Ghyll	37
*Whit's End Direct	Gimmer Crag	22

VERY SEVERE (HARD)

Adam's Apple	Neckband Crag	96
Andromeda	Pavey Ark	63
**Arcturus	Pavey Ark	53
B.B. Corner	Flat Crag, Bowfell	86
Beacon Rib	Helm Crag	109
Bleaberry Buttress	Blea Crag	112
Bradley's Damnation	Raven Crag	71
Brown Trousers	East Raven Crag	80
By-Pass Route	Pavey Ark	61
Cascade	Pavey Ark	68
Chequer Buttress	Pavey Ark	60
Chopper, The	East Raven Crag	80
**Deer Bield Crack	Deer Bield Crag	115
Dunmail Cracks	Deer Bield Crag	114
Ethics of War	White Ghyll	36
Festerday	East Raven Crag	79
Flarepath Direct	Helm Crag	110
Gamekeeper, The	Raven Crag	71
Gibli, The	North Buttress, Bowfell	88
**Girdle Traverse, The	Gimmer Crag	32
Gnomon	North Buttress, Bowfell	88
*Golden Slipper	Pavey Ark	57
*Grooves Superdirect	Gimmer Crag	29
*Grooves Traverse	Gimmer Crag	29
Inertia	Gimmer Crag	29
*Intern	Gimmer Crag	25
Jericho Wall	East Raven Crag	81
***Kipling Groove	Gimmer Crag	23
Kneewrecker Chimney	Raven Crag	76
**Laugh Not	White Ghyll	37
Little Corner	Pavey Ark	56
Mendes Traverse	Raven Crag	71
**Mithrandir	Neckband Crag	96
Muscle Crack	Raven Crag	77
Nutcracker Cleft	Raven Crag	76
Perhaps Not	White Ghyll	42
*Pluto	Raven Crag	74
*Poacher	Gimmer Crag	22
Rainbow	Helm Crag	110
**Razor Crack	Neckband Crag	96
Rectangular Rib	Pavey Ark	59
*Rib Pitch, The	Pavey Ark	62
Right Wall Eliminate	Bowfell Buttress	93
Rope Not	White Ghyll	40
Samarkand	East Raven Crag	82

VERY SEVERE (HARD) (continued)

Shroud, The	East Raven Crag	81
Sorbo	Blea Crag	111
Stickle Grooves	Pavey Ark	63
Swastika	North Buttress, Bowfell	89
Tapestry	White Ghyll	41
Troll's Corner	Pavey Ark	57
Virgo	Neckband Crag	95

VERY SEVERE

Alph	Pavey Ark	52
*Bilberry Buttress	Raven Crag	75
Carpetbagger	Gimmer Crag	30
Casket	East Raven Crag	80
***Crack, The	Gimmer Crag	27
Crescent Direct	Pavey Ark	52
Crossword	Spout Crag	107
Crows Nest Direct	Gimmer Crag	18
Damascus	East Raven Crag	82
Deuterus	Raven Crag, Walthwaite	105
Evening Oak Variations	Raven Crag	72
Flarepath	Helm Crag	110
Flat Crag Corner	Flat Crag, Bowfell	86
**'F' Route	Gimmer Crag	22
Girdle Traverse, The	East Raven Crag	83
Girdle Traverse, The	Neckband Crag	97
Girdle Traverse, The	Raven Crag, Walthwaite	106
Gizzard, The	Neckband Crag	95
**Gordian Knot	White Ghyll	42
Granny Knot Direct	White Ghyll	40
Gurt Gardin Stuff	Spout Crag	107
**Haste Not	White Ghyll	43
*Hiatus	Gimmer Crag	28
Hitcher	White Ghyll	40
*Holly Tree Direct	Raven Crag	73
Hot Pot	Raven Crag	78
Joas	Gimmer Crag	25
Mendes	Raven Crag	71
Moss Wall	White Ghyll	38
Nadir	Raven Crag	73
Ninevah	East Raven Crag	82
Protus	Raven Crag, Walthwaite	106
**Rake End Wall	Pavey Park	61
Ramrod	East Raven Crag	80
Rectangular Slab	Pavey Ark	58
Right Hand Wall	Bowfell Buttress	93
Roundabout Direct	Pavey Ark	56
Rowan Tree Groove	East Raven Crag	79
Runner Wall	White Ghyll	45
Salmon Leap	Scout Crag	101
Scabbard	North Buttress, Bowfell	89

VERY SEVERE (continued)

Shivering Timber	White Ghyll	38
Sign of Four	East Raven Crag	81
Stalag	Pavey Ark	58
Walthwaite Crack	Raven Crag, Walthwaite	105
White Ghyll Traverse	White Ghyll	46
Whit's End	Gimmer Crag	22

VERY SEVERE (MILD)

Ashen Traverse	Gimmer Crag	32
Barry's Traverse	Gimmer Crag	24
Baskerville	East Raven Crag	85
Bowfell Buttress Girdle	Bowfell Buttress	94
Cravat	Neckband Crag	97
Godiva Groove	Gimmer Crag	30
Jingo	East Raven Crag	79
Limpet Grooves	Side Pike	104
Nectar	Neckband Crag	95
Nocturne	Gimmer Crag	31
North West Arête	Gimmer Crag	25
Peascod's Route	East Raven Crag	83
Schizen Groove	East Raven Crag	80
**Slip Knot	White Ghyll	38
Wailing Wall	Pavey Ark	52
Walthwaite Gully	Raven Crag, Walthwaite	106
**White Ghyll Wall	White Ghyll	41

SEVERE (HARD)

Alfresco	Raven Crag, Walthwaite	105
**Asterisk	Gimmer Crag	26
Bachelor Crack	Gimmer Crag	16
Beacon Crack	Helm Crag	109
***Bracket and Slab Climb	Gimmer Crag	17
Central Route, The	Bowfell Buttress	91
Deer Bield Chimney	Deer Bield Crag	117
Diphthong	Gimmer Crag	19
Eden Groove	Deer Bield Crag	119
'E' Route	Gimmer Crag	20
Granny Knot	White Ghyll	40
Grondle Grooves	Gimmer Crag	15
*Hobson's Choice	Pavey Ark	66
Introduction	Gimmer Crag	24
Jungle Wall	Raven Crag	79
Lichen Groove	Gimmer Crag	20
Musgrave's Traverse	Gimmer Crag	21
Samaritan Corner	Gimmer Crag	26
Sinister Slabs	Bowfell Buttress	90
**Stoats' Crack	Pavey Ark	64
Watson Wall	East Raven Crag	81

SEVERE

Bluebell Arête	Raven Crag	78
Bluebell Gully	Raven Crag	77
Borstal Buttress	Cambridge Crag, Bowfell	87
Bracken Route	Pavey Ark	59
*Centipede	Raven Crag	78
Chimney Buttress	Gimmer Crag	16
Confidence	Raven Crag	78
*Crescent Slabs	Pavey Ark	51
Crescent Wall	Pavey Ark	51
*'C' Route	Gimmer Crag	19
Deception	Pavey Ark	55
**'D' Route	Gimmer Crag	21
Easedale Groove	Deer Bield Crag	118
Evening Wall	Raven Crag	72
Flat Crag Climb	Flat Crag, Bowfell	87
Grouter, The	Helm Crag	110
Hardup Wall	Raven Crag, Walthwaite	105
Heather Groove	White Ghyll	35
*Hollin Groove	White Ghyll	39
Hyphen	Gimmer Crag	21
Inferno	White Ghyll	36
Jaundice	Raven Crag	77
Junction Arête	White Ghyll	35
Marrawak	Side Pike	104
Monkey Puzzle	Deer Bield Crag	119
Not Again	White Ghyll	36
Ornithology	East Raven Crag	80
Pale Face	Gimmer Crag	31
*Pallid Slabs	Gimmer Crag	31
Pianissimo	East Raven Crag	81
*Raven Girdle	Raven Crag	77
*Revelation	Raven Crag	76
Roundabout	Pavey Ark	56
Route 1	Raven Crag, Walthwaite	105
Route 2	Raven Crag, Walthwaite	105
Russet Groove	White Ghyll	35
Siamese Chimneys	North Buttress, Bowfell	87
**Slabs, The, Route 1	White Ghyll	45
*Slabs, The, Route 2	White Ghyll	46
Stewpot	Raven Crag	78
Stony Buttress	Pavey Ark	49
Terrace Crack	Crinkle Crag	108
Walthwaite Chimney	Raven Crag, Walthwaite	105
*White Ghyll Chimney	White Ghyll	45

SEVERE (MILD)

**'A' Route	Gimmer Crag	19
**'B' Route	Gimmer Crag	19
Grey Corner	Bowfell Buttress	93
Grey Rib	Bowfell Buttress	94

SEVERE (MILD) (continued)

Juniper Buttress	Gimmer Crag	30
Ledge and Groove	Bowfell Buttress	92
Mamba	East Raven Crag	79
Oak Tree Wall	Raven Crag	72
Orchid	Tarn Crag	102
*Original Route	Raven Crag	73
Savernake	Raven Crag	75
Spider Crack	Side Pike	104
Tinning's Move	Side Pike	104
Wall End	Gimmer Crag	32

VERY DIFFICULT

*Ash-Tree Slabs	Gimmer Crag	25
Bentley	Helm Crag	110
Blandish	Tarn Crag	102
Blea Rigg Climb	Blea Crag	111
***Bowfell Buttress	Bowfell Buttress	91
Cartwheel	Gimmer Crag	24
Cook's Tour	Pavey Ark	59
Garden Path	White Ghyll	39
**Gimmer Chimney	Gimmer Crag	16
Harristickorner	Harrison Stickle	103
Heather Slab	Tarn Crag	102
Herdwick Buttress	Gimmer Crag	24
Holly Tree Crack	Helm Crag	109
*Holly Tree Traverse	Raven Crag	73
Interlude	Gimmer Crag	24
Main Wall Climb	Gimmer Crag	15
Mary Ann	Flat Crag, Bowfell	85
Neckband, The	Neckband Crag	95
**Oliverson's Variation and Lyon's Crawl	Gimmer Crag	20
Porphyry Slab	Harrison Stickle	103
Question Not	White Ghyll	39
Ramblers Hangover	Scout Crag	99
Rough Ridge	Side Pike	104
Route 1·5	Scout Crag	100
Scouts Belt	Scout Crag	100
Speckled Band	East Raven Crag	79
Subsidiary Ridge	East Raven Crag	81
Why Not	White Ghyll	39
Zero Route	Scout Crag	96

DIFFICULT (HARD)

Cambridge Climb, The	Cambridge Crag, Bowfell	87

DIFFICULT

*Great Gully	Pavey Ark	49
Gwynne's Chimney	Pavey Ark	58
Merlin Slab	Pike o' Stickle	103

DIFFICULT (continued)

*Middlefell Buttress	Raven Crag	70
Plaque Route, The	Bowfell Buttress	90
Prelude	Gimmer Crag	18
**Rake End Chimney	Pavey Ark	60
Rib and Wall	Tarn Crag	103
Route 1	Gibson Knott	111
*Route 1	Scout Crag	99
Route 1	Tarn Crag	103
Route 2	Gibson Knott	111
Route 2	Scout Crag	100
Route 2	Tarn Crag	102
South East Lower Traverse	Gimmer Crag	17
West Buttress	Tarn Crag	102

MODERATE

Crescent Climb	Pavey Ark	51
Little Gully	Pavey Ark	49

FIRST ASCENTS

Alternate and Varied leads are indicated respectively by (alt) and var).

1870/80	**Jack's Rake,** Date indefinite R Pendlebury
1882	**Great Gully,** Pavey Ark W P Haskett-Smith
1882	**North Gully,** Bowfell Buttress W P Haskett-Smith
1882	**North-west Gully,** Gimmer Crag W P Haskett-Smith
1886 June	**Little Gully,** Pavey Ark W P Haskett-Smith
1892 April	**Gwynne's Chimney** H A Gwynne and party

W P Haskett-Smith had previously descended the Chimney 18 March 1923. Variation. R S T Chorley, H P Cain, W G Pape.

1898 Oct 1	**Rake End Chimney** C W Barton
1902 May 24	**Bowfell Buttress** T Shaw, G H Craig, G R West, C Hargreaves and L J Oppenheimer

30 September 1916. Alternative start, H M Kelly 20 September 1919, Variation by Chimney, T H Somervell, L Somervell

1902 Nov 2	**Gimmer Chimney** E Rigby, J Sandison and A S Thomson

The more direct and severe chimney (see Bracket and Slab Climb), was climbed as an alternative by H M Kelly and J B Meldrum, 18 May 1918

1902 Nov 2	**South-east Lower Traverse,** Gimmer Crag E Rigby
1903 April 7	**'A' Route** E Rigby, D Leighton, J Sandison
1907 April	**Crescent Climb** F Botterill, W E Palmer

NB—The Gully portion of this climb was done by C W Barton, 24 October 1899

1907 May 26	**Oliverson's Variation** C H Oliverson, G C Turner, F B Kershaw
1907 May 26	**Lyon's Crawl** H B Lyon, J Stables, A S Thomson
1907 July 7	**'B' Route** H B Lyon, J Stables, A S Thomson
1907 Sept 22	**Junipall Gully** Fell and Rock Party, Names not recorded
1908 Oct	**Blea Rigg Climb** G C Turner, J Stables
1908 Oct	**Deer Bield Chimney** J Stables, G C Turner
1910 Mar 22	**Gibson's Chimney** H Bishop, C D Yeomans
1910 Mar 28	**Bennison's Chimney** W E Bennison, A E Burns, T H Seaton, C D Yeomans
1911 Sept 24	**Middlefell Buttress** J Laycock, S W Herford, A R Thomson
1918 Aug 3	**'C' Route** A P Wilson, G H Jackson, A Brundritt
1919 May 31	**'D' Route** G S Bower, P R Masson

Gritstone techniques introduced to Langdale by a Black Rocks expert

1920 April 18	**Stony Buttress** G S Bower, A W Wakefield
1920 June 19	**Crescent Slabs** G S Bower, A W Wakefield

1920 June 20 **Ash-tree Slabs** G S Bower, A W Wakefield
1921 Jan 30 **Harristickorner** G S Bower, J C Appleyard
1921 July 28 **Route 1,** Tarn Crag J A Garrick, W L Tulip
1922 June 8 **Juniper Buttress** C F Holland, A S Piggott, Morley Wood
1922 Sept 6 **Cambridge Climb** W T Elmslie, A de St C Walsh
1922 Oct **Routes 1 & 2,** Scout Crag F Graham
Variation Route 1, Easter 1957. R A Brayshaw, N K T Froggatt
Variation Route 2, 8 July 1950. J R Files, M Moxey
1923 Aug 8 **Bracket and Slab Climb** H B Lyon, J Herbert
1923 Aug 10 **White Ghyll Chimney** H B Lyon, J Herbert, H P Cain
10 April 1948. Variation to Pitch 2, J D Teare
1923 Sept 3 **Chimney Buttress** H B Lyon, G Ackerley, J Herbert
1924 Aug 11 **'E' Route** J A Wray, G Basterfield
1924 Aug 11 **Right-hand Wall,** Bowfell M de Selincourt, Miss B Ritchie
1924 Sept 1 **The Neckband** M de Selincourt
1924 Sept 7 **Holly-tree Crack,** Helm Crag M de Selincourt
1924 **Crescent Wall** M de Selincourt
1925 Mar 18 **Herdwick Buttress** F Graham
1925 April **Routes 1 & 2,** Gibson Knott A R Thomson, A Dibona
1926 May 13 **Pallid Slabs** G S Bower, A W Wakefield, H V Hughes
1926 June 27 **Diphthong** Morley Wood, G S Bower, A B Reynolds, F Frischmann
1927 July 10 **Hiatus** G S Bower, A B Reynolds, A W Wakefield, G G Macphee
First climbed on a rope from above by G Basterfield and J R Tyson in 1926
1931. Variation Finish, A W Bridge, A B Hargreaves
1928 May 5 **The Crack,** Gimmer Crag A B Reynolds, G G Macphee
4 April 1928. First ascended with a rope from above by A B Reynolds and H G Knight
1928 May 6 **Borstal Buttress** A B Reynolds, G G Macphee, R C Abbatt
1928 May 13 **Asterisk** H S Gross, G Basterfield, B Tyson
1928 **Joas** G G Macphee, A B Reynolds
1929 Aug 8 **Musgrave's Traverse** J A Musgrave, Miss N Ridyard
1930 Feb 16 **Deer Bield Crack** A T Hargreaves, G G Macphee
The party reported the climb to be Severe!
1930 Aug 10 **Original Route,** Raven Crag S Watson, D Usher, R Holmes, W Cowen, N Middleton
1930 Sept 15 **Route 1,** White Ghyll Slabs G Barker, A T Hargreaves

1931 April 30	**Plaque Route** H M Kelly, Blanche Eden-Smith
1931 May 20	**Central Route** H M Kelly, Blanche Eden-Smith
1932 Sept 24	**Sinister Slabs** A T Hargreaves, G G Macphee
1933 June 28	**Stoats' Crack** B R Record, J R Jenkins
	9 August 1945. Variation to pitch 3, H A Carsten, E H Phillips
1933 July 21	**Kettle Crag Climbs** J Wharton, F G Stangle
1933	**Route 2**, White Ghyll Slabs, S Cross, E Fallowfield, C Tatham
	21 August 1947. Alternative Start, A Gregory, J W Tucker
1936 Sept 21	**Barry's Traverse** R V M Barry, E G Harper
1936 Sept 21	**Grooves Traverse** R V M Barry, E G Harper
1938 April 17	**Hyphen** A Mullan, G Parkinson
1939 April 16	**Zero Route** S Thompson, J Diamond
1939 May 6	**Deception** S H Cross, Alice M Nelson
	September 1959. J A Austin, Miss J M Ruffe, Variation Start
1939 Aug 26	**Wailing Wall** S H Cross, A T Hargreaves, Ruth Hargreaves, Alice Nelson
1940	**Crow's Nest Direct** S Thompson, Phyllis White, A Mullan, Valerie Bolton, J Ashton
	13 January 1946. Alternative Start, A R Dolphin, A B Gilchrist
1940 April 18	**Prelude** A H Griffin, L K Griffin, J Diamond
1940 Sept 15	**North-west Arête** R J Birkett, V Veevers
1940 Sept 15	**The Gordian Knot** J W Haggas, Miss E Bull
1940 Sept 29	**Interlude** J Ashton, J Diamond, J Brady
1940 Oct 13	**Wall End** J Ashton, J Diamond, J Apted, Lyna Kellett
1940 Oct 13	**Paleface** J Ashton, J Apted, Lyna Kellett, J Diamond
1941 May 4	**'F' Route** R J Birkett, V Veevers
1941 June 27	**Bilberry Buttress** C F Rolland, J F Renwick
1941 Aug 3	**Bachelor Crack** R J Birkett, V Veevers, J Craven
1942 May	**Bowfell Buttress Girdle** S H Cross, A T Hargreaves, Ruth Hargreaves, Alice Cross
1942 June 17	**Bracken Route** G B Elliott, A Mullan, S A Williams
1942 Aug 11	**Porphyry Slab** J R Jenkins, J A Martinez, M S Taylor
1943 Mar 14	**Cook's Tour** J Cook, G B Elliott
	NB—The last two pitches were climbed as an extension to Gwynne's Chimney by G B Elliott and T Nicholson in September 1942
1943 Sept 5	**Savernake** J E Q Barford, M P Ward
1945 Feb 26	**Peascod's Route** W Peascod, J Pugh
1945 May 5	**Ledge and Groove** R D Stevens, G Stoneley
	The upper part had been climbed from the gully by G B Elliott and H M Elliott, 1 May 1942
1945 Aug 1	**Hollin Groove** R J Birkett, L Muscroft

1945 Aug 9 **Rake End Wall** H A Carsten, E H Phillips
1945 Sept 24 **Nocturne** A R Dolphin, J W Cook
14 April 1946. *Groove variation start, D D Davies, B Black*
22 April 1946. *Direct start, A R Dolphin, D D Davies, D C Birch*
1946 Jan 15 **Monkey Puzzle** A R Dolphin, A B Gilchrist
1946 May 5 **Ashen Traverse** D D Davies, J M Hirst
1946 May 9 **White Ghyll Wall** R J Birkett, L Muscroft, T Hill
1946 June 23 **White Ghyll Traverse** R J Birkett, L Muscroft, T Hill
1946 July 21 **Spider Crack** R Bumstead, D J Hewitt, R L Plackett
1947 May 25 **Slip Knot** R J Birkett, L Muscroft
1947 May 25 **Limpet Grooves** A R Dolphin, M Dwyer
1947 May 26 **Garden Path** A R Dolphin M Dwyer
1947 May 27 **Whit's End** A R Dolphin, M Dwyer
Pitch 3 was added by R Smith and J Moriarty, 1959
1947 June 23 **Protus** D C Birch, A R Dolphin
1947 June 23 **Deuterus** A R Dolphin, D C Birch, J W Cook
1947 July 12 **Oak-tree Wall** A Gregory, J Woods
1958. *Variation Finish, G Oliver, F Carrol, P Ross, A Campbell*
1947 July 12 **Cartwheel** J A Mullan, A C Cain, J Lancaster
1947 July 20 **Junction Arête** L Muscroft, R J Birkett
1947 Aug 10 **Heather Groove** R J Birkett, L Muscroft, J Craven
1947 Aug 31 **Hobson's Choice** J W Cook, A R Dolphin (alt)
1947 Sept 4 **Scout's Belt** J Lancaster, E Kelly A C Cain
1947 Oct 4 **Route 1·5** R A Ewin, J R Files
1947 Oct 6 **Evening Wall** A Gregory, J W Tucker, J Woods
1955. *Variation Start, E Metcalf*
1948 Mar 13 **Raven Girdle** A Gregory, J Ward, J W Tucker
1948 Mar 29 **Revelation** A Gregory, B Black, J Woods
1948 April 23 **Introduction** D J Cameron, A B Durrant
1948 May 9 **Haste Not** R J Birkett, L Muscroft
1948 May 15 **Samaritan Corner** A R Dolphin, J B Lockwood, J Bloor
1948 May 16 **Alph** A R Dolphin, J B Lockwood, J Bloor
14 July 1971. *Variation pitch 2, D M Hardwick, J Mitchell, J Greybrook*
23 April 1972. *Direct start, D Miller, J A Austin, R Matheson*
1948 May 17 **Kipling Groove** A R Dolphin, J B Lockwood
First ascended on a top rope. Much bolder in conception than its contemporaries. The climb was a remarkable lead for the period
1948 May 23 **Granny Knot** R J Birkett, L Muscroft
2 September 1971. *Direct start, R Sager, R Meakin, G Thompson*
1948 May 29 **Bluebell Gully** A Gregory, J W Tucker, J Ward, C Peckett

1948 July 10	**Centipede** A Gregory, C Peckett	
1948 Sept 4	**Rambler's Hangover** W Kelsie, D McKelvie	
1948 Sept 18	**Bluebell Arête** A Gregory, J Renwick	
1948 Dec 12	**Route 2,** Tarn Crag A Gregory, J Renwick	
1949 Feb 6	**Why Not** L Muscroft, R J Birkett (alt)	
1949 April 24	**Watson Wall** A R Dolphin, J Bloor	
1949 April 24	**Baskerville** A R Dolphin, J Bloor	
1949 May 2	**Lichen Groove** A C Cain, J Lancaster	

NB—A route closely corresponding to this was climbed solo by J M Edwards some ten years before, but could not be identified exactly

1949 May 15	**Perhaps Not** R J Birkett, L Muscroft (alt)	
1949 June 4	**Grey Corner** R D Stevens, Mrs J Stevens	
1949 June 5	**Grey Rib** R D Stevens, Mrs J Stevens	
1949 June 7	**Kneewrecker Chimney** A R Dolphin, J Bloor	
1949 June 19	**Do Not** R J Birkett, L Muscroft	

This was the second pitch only, climbed as an alternative finish to Slip Knot. The independent start was added by K. Heaton and A Heaton on 9 October 1949, and the direct start by L Brown and P Muscroft 29 October 1960; a foot loop was used on the 10-foot crack.

1949 June 25	**Nectar** K Heaton, J Umpleby, J A Jackson	
1949 June 26	**Stewpot** A Gregory, A R Dolphin	
1949 June 27	**Heather Slab** J W Cook	
1949 July 3	**Rib and Wall** A Gregory, J Woods	
1949 July 3	**Orchid** A Gregory, J Woods, J Renwick	
1949 July 3	**Blandish** A Gregory, J Woods, J Renwick	
1949 Aug 28	**Grooves Superdirect** A R Dolphin, J Bloor	

Pitch 1 added 3 July 1970 by M Mortimer and J A Austin

The groove direct by M Mortimer, Easter 1976

1949 Aug 28	**West Buttress,** Tarn Crag A Gregory, J Woods	
1949 Sept 4	**Gimmer Girdle** A R Dolphin, J W Cook	

The outcome of much wandering. On the 5 July a complete traverse of the Crag had been achieved by J W Cook, J G Ball and L J Griffin, following an easier, and inferior, line across the NW face via the second pitch of Godiva Groove

1949 Sept 7	**Neckband Girdle** K Heaton, S Vernon	
1949 Sept 18	**Russet Groove** A R Dolphin, K Heaton (alt)	
1949 Sept 18	**Inferno** K Heaton, A R Dolphin (alt)	
1949 Oct 8	**The Gizzard** K Heaton, A Heaton	
1950 Jan 7	**Godiva Groove** C M G Smith, L J Griffin	
1950 July 1	**Question Not** C Peckett, J Renwick	
1950	**Cravat** H Drasdo, N Drasdo	
1951 Oct 7	**Rubicon Groove** A R Dolphin, A D Brown	

Well named! A remarkably bold first ascent

1951 June 24	**Deer Bield Buttress** A R Dolphin, A D Brown	

A. R. D.'s solution to a long standing problem. El Dorado Variation, J Eastham, E Cleasby, 30 July 1977

1952 April 20 **Chequer Buttress** A R Dolphin, A D Brown
The party traversed into Rake End Chimney just above the little slab for a belay, and returned along the Girdle. The route was not popular and it was not until 1965 that a new way was found.
21 *June* 1970. *Variation finish, M Bebbington, J A Austin, S Wood*

1952 July 27 **Holly Tree Direct** H Drasdo, E Mallinson
31 *August* 1963. *The Overhang Direct, J A Austin, E Metcalf*

1952 Aug 16 **Shivering Timber** A R Dolphin, J Wilkinson

1952 Aug 23 **Sword of Damocles** P J Greenwood, D Hopkin, A R Dolphin (alt)
A. R. D. led pitch 2
It was not thought that the 'Sword' would last long. In fact it remained for another 26 years

1952 Aug 24 **Dunmail Cracks** P J Greenwood, A R Dolphin (alt), V N Stephenson

1952 Sept 4 **Bradley's Damnation** P Woods, P J Greenwood (alt)

1952 **Nutcracker Cleft** V Ridgeway, P J Greenwood (alt)

1953 Feb 2 **Mendes** P Woods, J Sutherland

1953 May 31 **Pendulum** R Moseley
Moseley abseiled down to place a piton, used for aid Climbed free, E Cleasby, 23 June 1977

1953 July 9 **Not Again** T Parker, M Dawson, A C Cain

1953 Oct 3 **Dight** R Moseley, R Greenall
The party started out from the Bower and completed their ascent unaware that only the first half was new. The top pitch had been led by A R D as part of the Girdle. The modern way on pitch 2 was climbed by J A Austin and E Metcalf, 25 May 1963. Pitch 1 and the variations were added by G Gibson and D Beetlestone, August 1979

1953 Oct 17 **Laugh Not** J Brown, R Moseley, T Waghorn
A tension traverse was used to cross the slab under the big roof

1953 Oct 18 **Girdle of Deer Bield Crag** D Whillans, R Moseley

1953 Oct 25 **Girdle of Raven Crag**, Walthwaite A C Cain, R Brooks, R Miller

1953 **Terrace Crack**, Crinkle Crags D M Oxtoby, R L Lockwood

1954 Feb 6 **Alfresco** A C Cain, P J Greenwood

1954 Mar 28 **Flarepath** P J Greenwood, A C Cain

1954 Mar 28 **Bentley** D Ball, P J Greenwood, A C Cain

1956 Jan 5 **Hubris** H Drasdo, A J Norton
An epic ascent! Pitons were used for both aid and protection. A young sapling which fortuitously hung down over the crux is, alas, no longer with us

1956 April 14	**Stickle Grooves** J A Austin, R B Evans (alt)
1956 May 27	**Eden Groove** R B Evans, J A Austin (alt)
1957 Mar 3	**Grondle Grooves** C R Allen, N J Soper (alt)
1957 May 18	**Walthwaite Gully** J A Austin, Miss J M Ruffe
1957 May 26	**Cascade** J A Austin, R B Evans
1957	**Eliminot** J Brown, J Smith

*On pitch 2 the team traversed the long
'sandwiched' slab to join up with White Ghyll Wall.
The overhang exit was found by J A Austin and
I Roper on 14 August 1966*

1957 Nov 9	**Marrawhack** F Holmes, M Cheevers
1958 June 1	**By-pass Route** J A Austin, Miss J M Ruffe

*Easter 1971. Variation pitch 3, R Valentine, P L
Fearnehough*

1958 June 1	**The Rib Pitch** J A Austin, Miss J M Ruffe
1958 June 29	**Stalag** J A Austin, R B Evans (alt)
1958 June 29	**Roundabout** R B Evans, J A Austin (alt)
1958 July 19	**Golden Slipper** J A Austin, R B Evans
1958 July	**Salmon Leap** A H Greenbank, M Thompson
1958 Summer	**Pluto** A L Atkinson

*Only the first pitch was new; the middle pitch had
been led by P Woods, 2 January 1953 and was
known as M and B Traverse. Pitch 3 had been
climbed by E Metcalf and J Ramsden in 1957 as a
finish to Bilberry Buttress. Green Groove finish was
climbed by R Matheson and M Matheson, Summer
1972*

1959 May 2	**Virgo** G Oliver, F Carrol
1959 Aug 8	**Moss Wall** G Oliver, D Laws

*A cunning solution to a problem which had baffled
tigers for years*

1959 Aug 26	**Inertia** L Brown, R G Wilson

*The party traversed left on what was to become the
Girdle to finish up Grooves Superdirect. The second
pitch was added 25 May 1963 by E Metcalf and
J A Austin*

1959 Sept	**Beacon Rib** D G Farley, B A Fuller
1959 Sept 20	**Trolls Corner** J A Austin, Miss J M Ruffe
1960 April 23	**Gnomon** L Brown, G Lund
1960 May 2	**Mendes Traverse** B Kershaw, R Brown
1960 May 20	**Rectangular Slab**, Pavey Ark J A Austin, E Metcalf

E. M. led pitch 1

1960 May 27	**Astra** J A Austin, E Metcalf (alt) D G Roberts

A piton was used for aid

1960 May 28	**The Scabbard** J A Austin, E Metcalf (alt)
1960 May 28	**Flat Crag Corner** E Metcalf, J A Austin (alt) D G Roberts
1960 July 3	**Red Groove** J A Austin E Metcalf

*The party attempted to traverse left from the niche
using pitons and tension!*

1960	**Hitcher** N Drasdo, F P Jenkinson
1961 May 14	**Easedale Groove** R B Evans, L S Howell, Mrs A Evans
1962 April 28	**Arcturus** J A Austin, E Metcalf (var)
1963 May 18	**Swastika** J A Austin, E Metcalf (alt)
1963 May 26	**Intern** P Fearneough, J Oliver, J Hesmondhalgh

The first pitch only. The second pitch was climbed by J A Austin and I Roper, 19 March 1966

1963 Whit	**The Gibli** N J Soper, J A Austin (alt)
1963 July 15	**Gimmer String** J A Austin, E Metcalf, D Miller

All the pitches had been climbed previously:—the Direct Start to Kipling Groove had been led by J Brown in 1952; the Rib had been climbed from the Crack with the aid of a piton; R Smith and J Moriarty had linked KG and the Rib with the aid of another piton. It only remained to remove the pitons and string it together

1963 July 21	**Poacher** J A Austin, E Metcalf (alt)
1963 Nov 18	**Rough Ridge** A H Greenbank, J A Austin
1964 June 21	**Bowfell Buttress Eliminate** J A Austin, D G Roberts

Earlier in the year R B Evans and A H Greenbank had climbed the Girdle as far as the Rib. The Direct Finish was climbed by P Livesey in 1975

1964 July 4	**Gandalf's Groove** J A Austin, F P Jenkinson
1964 July 5	**Sorbo** N J Soper, J A Austin (alt)
1964 July 12	**Bleaberry Buttress** J A Austin, N J Soper (alt) D G Roberts
1965 April 3	**Man of Straw** J A Austin, D G Roberts

The lower level exit was first led by J Syrett in 1970 rendering the use of a piton at the top of the groove unnecessary

1965 July 10	**Rainmaker** J A Austin, I Roper, A H Greenbank

A piton was used for aid

1966 April 30	**Chimney Variant** J A Austin, I Roper, D Miller
1966 April 30	**Roundabout Direct** J A Austin, D Miller, I Roper, H Wiggins
1966 July 16	**Poker Face** J A Austin, K Wood
1966 Aug 6	**Variation Traverse**, White Ghyll Crag J A Austin, K Wood (alt)
1966 Aug 26	**Razor Crack** J A Austin, K Wood
1967 Summer	**The Grouter** J A Austin, I Roper (alt)
1967 July 22	**The Gamekeeper** D Harding, E Grindley

A similar line was climbed in this area by B Kershaw circa 1960

1968 June 9	**Carpetbagger** N Allinson, N J Soper (alt)
1968 July 7	**Peccadillo** C Read, J Adams

Two points of aid and a preplaced peg and sling for aid. Climbed free by P Botterill and S Clegg, 29 May 1977

1968 July	**Gillette** K Wood, J A Austin

1969 Direct Finish, W Lounds

1968 Aug 2   **Andromeda**   N J Soper, N Allinson (alt)
*On the first ascent the party climbed the first 20
feet of Stoats' Crack, before swinging onto the wall*

1969 May 18   **Crescent Direct**   J A Austin, D G Roberts

1969 July   **Rainbow**   R D Barton, J L Cardy

1969 Summer **The Hobbit**   J Fullalove, R Wood

1969 Aug 17   **BB Corner**   K Wood, F Booth

1970 June 14 **The Bracken-clock**   J A Austin, N J Soper, Miss A
Faller
*Named after an insect (phyllopertha porticola),
which was infesting the crag on that day
A piton was used on pitch 2, but this pitch was led
free by R Valentine the following year*

1970 June 21 **Little Corner**   J A Austin, M Bebbington, S Wood

1970 July 7   **Crossword**   E Cross, N J Soper (alt)

1970 July 7   **Gurt Gardin Stuff**   N J Soper, E Cross (alt)

1970 Sept 26   **Paladin**   R Matheson
*Considerable aid was used on the first ascent but
the route was climbed free subsequently by R
Matheson*

1971 May 2   **The Ragman's Trumpet**   R Valentine, J A Austin

1971 May 2   **Haste Not Direct**   J A Austin, R Valentine
*The first complete ascent. Pitch 1 had been climbed
as a direct start to Haste Not by P Allison and N
Smithers in 1962. Pitch 2 was added by J A Austin
and C E Davies, 4 July 1965*

1971 May 9   **White Ghyll Eliminate**   A Evans, D Parker, G
Miller
*A sling was used for aid on the first ascent, but was
dispensed with by J A Austin the following April
during work for the guide*

1971 Summer **Sally Free and Easy**   P Livesey
One point of aid was used

1971 Summer **Mary Ann**   J Umpleby, P Grindley, J Slockett

1971 July 14 **The Graduate**   R Matheson, G Fleming, J Poole
(alt)
*Two points of aid were used, one of which was a
pre-placed peg and sling. The route had been
climbed previously but not recorded because
considerable aid had been used. The first free ascent
was made by J Lamb and P Smith, 19 June 1979*

1971 July 18 **Flat Iron Wall**   J A Austin, F Wilkinson (alt)

1971 Aug 10   **Sinistral**   P Long, S Michniewski

1971 Sept 4   **Slip Knot Variations**   H I Banner, D Ladkin
A point of aid was used on each pitch

1971 Sept   **Aragorn**   A Evans, D Parker
Two points of aid were used

1971 Sept 14 **Cascade Direct**   P Long, A D Barley
*Three points of aid were used. First free ascent was
made by P Whillance and J Moore in 1973*

1972 April 20 **Cruel Sister**   R Matheson, S Colvin
A controversial ascent because one of the two points of aid used was a pre-placed peg with a long sling. The first free ascent was by J Lamb and P Botterill, 19 February 1975

1972 May 20 **Tapestry**   R Matheson, M R Matheson, N B Lett

1972 June **Fine Time**   P Livesey, J Hammond
Yet another pre-placed peg and sling for aid! The upper half is a free version of the old aid route Kaisergebirge Wall. First completely free ascent, P Botterill, J Lamb, 23 June 1979

1972 Aug **Mithrandir**   J Hartley, R Sager

1972 Sept **Risus**   E Grindley, N J Soper, D J Harding

1972 Sept 22 **Dinsdale**   T W Birkett, M R Myers
One point of aid was used. The climb has become much harder since the removal of a block

1972 Sept 29 **Spiny Norman**   T W Birkett, R Gill
Much aid was used. The first free ascent was by M Berzins and B Berzins in 1976

1972 Sept 30 **Aardvark**   P Long, D J Harding
One point of aid was used. Named in the hope that it would be the first route in alphabetical order

1972 Oct 2 **Whit's End Direct**   J A Austin, R Valentine

1972 Oct 21 **Fallen Angel**   E Grindley, I Roper (alt)
A peg for aid and a peg for a rest were used on the main pitch. The first free ascent was by J Lamb and P Botterill in April 1974

1973 Aug 23 **Brain Damage**   E Grindley, G Higginson, P Long
A peg for resting was used on pitch 2

1973 Aug 25 **Mindprobe**   K Myhill, K Jones

1973 Sept 9 **Pearls Before Swine**   P Long, D J Harding

1974 Mar 31 **Tattered Banners**   P Long, E Grindley (var)
A number of falls were necessary

1974 Spring **Adam's Apple**   J Adams, R Valentine, P Long

1974 May 22 **Eastern Hammer**   P Livesey, A Manson
Replaces the old aid route If, climbed by P Ross in 1960

1974 June 22 **Efrafa**   E Grindley, J A Austin, T Parker
Better use of the available rock than Swordblade, climbed by A D Barley and R Barley, a route which it replaces

1974 Oct 13 **Rectangular Rib**   M G Mortimer, M G Allen

1975 June 15 **Right Wall Eliminate**   T W Birkett, E Cleasby (alt)
One point of aid on pitch 2

1976 April 21 **Equus**   E Cleasby
The alternative finish was added by M G Mortimer and M G Allen shortly afterwards, though part of this had been climbed earlier by G Cram

1976 April 26 **Eclipse**   P Whillance, P Botterill, S Clegg
One sling for resting was used on pitch 1

1976 May 8 **Gimmer High Girdle**   *M G Mortimer, M G Allen*

1976 June 26	**Startrek** M Berzins, B Berzins (alt)	
1976 July 3	**Breaking Point** P Livesey, J Sheard, J Lawrence, G Price	

The first pitch had been climbed earlier by E Cleasby and M Lynch

1976 July 8   **Mother Courage**   E Cleasby, R Matheson
A peg was used for a rest

1977 April 17   **Gymslip**   D Armstrong, P Whillance (alt)

1977 May 1   **R 'n' S Special**   G Summers, E Cleasby
One point of aid was used

1977 May 14   **Enormous Room**   M Berzins, B Berzins

1977 May 26   **Kudos**   P Sanson, W Lounds

1977 May   **Big Brother**   R Fawcett, C Gibb, I Edwards

1977 June 1   **Desperado**   P Whillance, D Armstrong

1977 June 4   **Warrior**   E Cleasby, R Matheson
The Rampant Finish was climbed with much aid by A Evans in 1972
Climbed free, summer 1978 by M Berzins and C Sowden

1977 June 5   **The Rib**   M G Mortimer, M G Allen

1977 June 18   **Solstice**   M Berzins, B Berzins
One rest sling was used

1977 June   **Waste-Not, Want-Not**   W Lounds, P Sanson

1977 July 16   **Obscured by Clouds**   P Whillance, D Armstrong

1977 July 19   **Imagination**   E Cleasby, R Matheson
A controversial ascent. The route was top-roped prior to leading

1978 April 4   **Stiletto**   P Whillance, D Armstrong

1978 May 6   **The New Girdle,** Deer Bield Crag   D Armstrong, P Whillance (alt)

1978 May 13   **Cut-throat**   M Berzins, B Berzins

1978 May 21   **Death Star**   T W Birkett, J Adams
The first pitch was protected by a runner pre-placed high in Rake End Chimney

1978 June 3   **Feet of Clay**   M G Mortimer, S Foster, M G Allen

1978 June 24   **Tinning's Move**   A Evans, G Milburn (alt), J Moran

1978 July 14   **Solaris**   M Berzins, C Sowden

1978 July 15   **Take it to the Limit**   P Whillance, D Armstrong (alt)

1978 July 16   **Flying Blind**   T W Birkett, K W Forsythe

1978 Summer   **Heartsong**   R Fawcett, C Gibb

1978 Summer   **The Horror**   R Fawcett
The first free ascent of the old aid route by P Ross

1979 May 30   **Trilogy**   J Lamb, E Cleasby
The first complete, free ascent. Originally an aid route by G West, I Hadfield and R Hughes, Easter 1957. Climbed free to an escape left below the big overhang by D Hollows and J Peel, 1977

1979 June 1	**Spring Bank** M G Mortimer, E Cleasby (var), M G Allen, M Lynch, J Lamb	
1979 June 1	**Poacher Right Hand** M G Mortimer, M G Allen *Incorporates the original finish to Poacher by E Metcalf and J A Austin, 21 July 1963*	
1979 June 10	**Karma** E Cleasby, I Greenwood	
1979 June 10	**Mindbender** R Kenyon, R Bennett	
1979 June 11	**Wilkinson's Sword** R Fawcett, C Gibb	
1979 June	**Fastburn** E Cleasby, I Greenwood	
1979 June/July	**Coma** J Lamb, P Botterill (var)	
1979 July 11	**Slowburn** B Berzins, M Berzins	
1979 July 12	**Ataxia** M Berzins, B Berzins	
1979 Aug 10	**Armalite** E Cleasby, R Matheson *Two routes were climbed higher up the gully by the same party on the same day*	
1979 August	**Dead Loss Angeles** G Gibson, D Beetlestone	
1979 Summer	**Supernova** R Fawcett, C Gibb	

MOUNTAIN ACCIDENTS

Procedure for Climbers in the Lake District
There has recently been considerable change in the procedures for mountain rescue in the Lake District. This change has been brought about by many factors, including the increase in the number and availability of rescue teams, the developments and improvements in equipment and techniques, and the increased availability (thanks to the R.A.F.) of helicopters for mountain rescue purposes.

Consequently, only minor casualties should come within the scope of treatment and evacuation by the climber's companions. The rule for all other cases is to make the casualty safe, to initiate the treatment, and to send expeditiously for a Mountain Rescue Team.

Sending for Help
A reliable member of the party should be sent for the Rescue Team, with full information about the nature of the injuries and the position of the incident (including, if possible, the map reference). **He should then find the nearest telephone, dial 999, and ask for the Police,** who will notify the most readily available team. The sender of the message should stay by the telephone until he receives instructions from the Team Leader, who may want further information or may want his help to guide the team to the incident.

General Treatment
Pending the arrival of the rescue team, basic first-aid treatment should be given. The patient should be examined as far as is possible without unduly exposing him. Wounds should be covered and external bleeding controlled by pressure of dressings. Application of tourniquets can be very dangerous and often make haemorrhage worse; they should only be used by experts and then only in extreme cases. Fractures should be immobilised by the most simple method available. The patient, if shocked, or suffering from actual or potential exposure, should then be put in a sheltered place, protected from the rain and wind, wrapped in as many layers of clothing as possible, encased in a 'poly-bag' or other impermeable material, and, if conscious and not suffering from abdominal injuries, given warm drinks containing glucose. If available a tent should be erected round him.

The majority of cases will respond to this treatment and their condition should have improved by the time the team arrives. The more serious cases, where such an improvement may not occur, include head injuries, spinal fractures, chest and abdominal injuries with possible internal haemorrhage, and multiple injuries with consequent severe shock. They require urgent expert treatment, and every effort should be made to stress the urgency and the nature of the injuries when the 999 call is made. The use of a helicopter, by courtesy of the R.A.F., can be quickly obtained through the Mountain Rescue Team Leader and the Police.

Treatment of special cases

Fractures of the limbs are usually best treated, in the case of the arm, by padding it and bandaging it to the chest, and in the case of the leg, by padding it and bandaging it to the other leg.

Severe head injuries run the risk of death from asphyxia with deepening unconsciousness. The position of the patient, his head and tongue should be adjusted to facilitate breathing. Apparently less severe head injuries should be continually and carefully observed as the condition of the patient can rapidly deteriorate.

Fracture of the spine, if suspected, means that the patient should *not* be moved and should be made to keep still. If he is in a dangerous position, a difficult decision will have to be made as to whether or not to move him. If he has to be moved to save his life, then obviously every care should be taken to prevent movement of the spine.

Internal haemorrhage should be suspected if the patient has sustained blows to the chest or abdomen. It is confirmed if, despite the measures adopted for the treatment and prevention of shock, his condition progressively deteriorates. All steps should be taken to facilitate the rapid arrival of doctor, team and, if possible, helicopter. A record should be kept of pulse rate to facilitate subsequent diagnosis.

Lack of help. The most difficult decision has to be made when the patient is severly injured, possibly unconscious, and there is only one climbing companion present. He should try to summon help from nearby climbers or walkers by shouting, giving the distress call on his whistle, flashing a torch, or sending up a red flare. If there is no response then he has to assess the relative dangers of leaving the patient, or of failing to get help, and should act decisively in the interest of the patient.

168

INDEX